YOU DESERVE TO BE HEARD

101 tips to boost your public speaking confidence

KERRY PIENAAR

Copyright © Kerry Pienaar 2022

All rights reserved. No part of this book may be used or reproduced by any means, graphic, electronic, or mechanical, including photocopying, recording, taping or by any information storage retrieval system without the written permission of the publisher except in the case of brief quotations embodied in critical articles and reviews.

Copies of this book can be ordered via the author's website at www.completecommunicationcoach.com.au, booksellers or by contacting:

*DoctorZed Publishing
10 Vista Ave, Skye,
South Australia 5072
www.doctorzed.com*

*ISBN: 978-0-6453427-1-0 (hc)
ISBN: 978-0-6453427-3-4 (sc)
ISBN: 978-0-6453427-2-7 (e)*

A CiP number is available at the National Library of Australia.

Because of the dynamic nature of the Internet, any web addresses or links contained in this book may have changed since publication and may no longer be valid. The views expressed in this work are solely those of the author and do not necessarily reflect the views of the publisher, and the publisher hereby disclaims any responsibility for them.

The author of this book does not dispense medical advice or prescribe the use of any technique as a form of treatment for physical, emotional, or medical problems without the advice of a physician, either directly or indirectly. The intent of the author is only to offer information of a general nature. In the event you use any of the information in this book for yourself, which is your constitutional right, the author and the publisher assume no responsibility for your actions.

*Cover image © Sergey Khakimullin
Part I (© Lightfieldstudiosprod), Part II (© Gpointstudio) & Part III (© Iakov Filimonov) images, Dreamstime.com
Author & Open palm images © Bob Stanford
Online meeting image: individual images © Pexels.com and compilation © Johnny Rizk
Avoid standing in front of the screen image © Vadymvdrobot, Dreamstime.com
Power Posing image © Johnny Rizk*

Printed in Australia, UK and USA

rev. date: 12/02/2022

DEDICATION

This book is dedicated to my husband Leonard and son Oliver, who have patiently and generously supported me to follow my passion for helping others with public speaking and communication. Love you guys.

CONTENTS

Praise for *You Deserve to Be Heard* vi
About the Author viii
Foreword x
Introduction xii

PART I: Understanding your fear 1
    1   You can overcome fear and self-doubt 3
    2   Managing your fear 10

PART II: Taking control 27
    3   Create connections and build trust 29
    4   Bring your voice to life 49

PART III: You deserve to be heard 63
    5   In a meeting 66
    6   At job interviews 75
    7   As a presenter 84
    8   On online platforms 100
    9   At social events 118
    10   As an MC 132
    11   At networking events 140
    12   As a technical presenter 160
    13   As a leader 172

Conclusion 182
Acknowledgements 184
Bibliography 186

PRAISE FOR 'YOU DESERVE TO BE HEARD'

'This book deserves to be read! *You Deserve to Be Heard* is far more than a book about public speaking. Kerry provides many tips that will make you a more effective communicator in your professional and personal life.

I'm looking forward to reaching for my copy in times of need; to help guide and reassure me through my many speaking and presenting occasions, big and small. There is so much to learn and so many opportunities to improve.'

**Michael Shearer,
General Manager, Coopers Brewery**

'No matter what stage you are at with public speaking and communication skills, everyone can find something to take home from this book. This valuable resource explodes with highly sought-after secrets, that are relatable, well written, and brimming full of descriptive engaging advice.

A delightful read where you can feel the emotion as author Kerry Pienaar shares her personal story of facing her fears to realising confidence and success. Easy to read, poignant and encouraging, enabling you to be heard.

A book that continues to give, keep this one handy you won't be sorry.'

**Sue Pederick,
Toastmasters International Past District Director,
District Education and Training coordinator and
Distinguished Toastmaster.**

'If you fear public speaking, this book is a must-read.

Kerry Pienaar shares a wealth of expertise and many inspiring client stories. The book takes the reader on a holistic journey from understanding and facing their fears to empowering techniques and strategies to use whenever and wherever they communicate. This includes high stakes meetings, job interviews or presentations face to face and online.

As one of Kerry's clients, I encourage you to implement the tips in this book - it will be life-changing. You will be well on your way to achieve what had seemed impossible until now.'

Elodie Janvier,
Strategic Research Development Manager

'This is the book all women wanting to gain confidence in speaking up and out need in their life. The format means that no matter what stage you are at, you will gain a new piece of knowledge to grow. Not only has Kerry provided the theory, but the real-world examples bring it all together. This is a book to read more than once; it's a handbook to pull out any time you need the confidence to stand up and be heard.'

Carly Thompson-Barry,
Founder and Business Nurturer, SA Woman

ABOUT THE AUTHOR

Recognised by Yahoo! Finance as one of Australia's top public speaking coaches in 2021, Kerry Pienaar's mission is for her clients to walk out the door feeling more confident than when they arrived.

Based in Adelaide, Kerry is a highly sought-after communication coach with a wealth of knowledge and experience. Working with individuals and groups with a diversity of challenges, Kerry's aim is to work with clients to identify and build upon strengths and conquer those fears and doubts that hold them back. Her solutions are both well-tested and personalised as she tailors to each client's individual needs and concerns.

She has coached TEDx Adelaide speakers and has provided support to government, corporate, and not-for-profit organisations. She has also run workshops for women to build their confidence, to encourage their participation in STEM programs and to pursue leadership careers.

Kerry has been recognised many times in state and Australian public speaking and coaching contests. As a Toastmasters International member, she won the evaluation championship at the highest level in Australia in 2015 and 2019.

About the author

Kerry wrote *You Deserve to Be Heard* to celebrate all she has learnt as a coach and public speaker. She is excited to share the stories of many of her clients who have made significant changes to their lives. They have faced their fears and put themselves out of their comfort zones to learn, move forward and pursue their dreams.

FOREWORD

Wow! Having spent a lifetime of public speaking, presenting and lecturing, I only wish I had access to the information presented in this book many years ago.

I worked with Kerry twenty years ago at the South Australian Tourism Commission where I was CEO and I have been absolutely delighted to have witnessed her journey and achievements since then. From Evaluation District Champion at Toastmasters International to a sought-after coach, Kerry assists others to develop their confidence as effective communicators when presenting, networking or undertaking interviews. In 2021, Kerry was recognised by Yahoo! Finance as one of Australia's top public speaking coaches.

Everyone has wonderful, inspiring, and captivating ideas and stories to share but many often find themselves held back by self-doubt, fear of failure or a perception that they aren't good enough.

Kerry's mission to support her clients to 'walk out the door' feeling more confident than when they arrived is an inspiring theme for this book. Kerry introduces you to the same techniques she gives her clients. 'You Deserve to be Heard' includes stories, case studies and 101 public-speaking tips that will see you embracing public presentations rather than dreading them.

FOREWORD

One of the inspirational stories outlined in the book says it all:

'Kerry helped me to change the way I think about public speaking. I went from dreading public speaking to embracing the challenge. She helped me work on my gestures, tone, energy and the way I shared my information. We also worked on managing nerves, breathing and anxiety. It helped my career profile so much. A few sessions with Kerry really did help me for life'.

No matter what stage of life you're in, you will relate to and benefit from the stories and tips outlined in Kerry's book, to assist you to become a more effective speaker, presenter and communicator.

What a great contribution Kerry has made and continues to make in changing people's lives.

W. T. (Bill) Spurr AO

Bill Spurr was awarded an 'Officer of the Order of Australia' in 2015 for 'distinguished service to tourism, to education, particularly through international marketing, to the arts and sport administration of institutions and events, and to the community of South Australia'.

INTRODUCTION

In 2017, my public speaking and communication coaching business, Complete Communication Coach, was born.

It's given me amazing opportunities to meet and coach hundreds of people from many walks of life who all have one thing in common; a terrible fear of public speaking.

My clients all share something else: their desire to be heard grew stronger than their fears. They succeeded because of their brave decision to do something about it. This book is full of success stories of people who now communicate with confidence.

All of my clients have wonderful, inspiring, innovative ideas and stories to share, but have found themselves held back by their self-doubt, fear of failure, or a perception that they aren't good enough. When we avoid sharing our stories and ideas, or when they're shared with a limited audience, or if our stories aren't shared with the power, passion, and influence they deserve, everyone misses out.

I've been privileged to have been part of their stories. This book has been written for people like them. If you're a person who wants to change, who wants a helping hand to move forward and to conquer your lifelong barrier of fear, I'm on your side. The tips and tools in my book are for you.

You deserve to be heard, and the world deserves to hear from you.

My story

My first public speaking experience is such a vivid memory. I was the tender age of five. The adults around me told me I was smart. Reading and spelling came easily, and therefore it was assumed I ought to have been able to present myself orally with just as much ease and confidence. The truth is, the thought of speaking publicly terrified me, but I didn't want to disappoint those who thought I was 'smart' enough to achieve anything.

When I was asked to recite a poem at a concert, I agreed hesitantly. I rehearsed the poem 'Mr Nobody' (anonymous) hundreds of times. On the day of the concert, dressed in my brand-new presentation dress, accessorised with shiny red shoes, I walked onto the stage with absolute trepidation. The sea of faces staring at me in the audience were a blur.

As I recited the first verse of the poem, my face burned red with fear and embarrassment:

'I know a funny little man, as quiet as a mouse,' … and then I ran off the stage crying.

That little five-year-old version of me was crushed, humiliated and devastated.

I carried that memory and feeling of failure through my school years. Whenever I had to speak publicly, despite some instances of success, I chose to hold on to my fear. Year 9 English included a unit on debating. Leading up to my first debate, I was terrified but could feel the support from the audience, and halfway through, I began to enjoy it. The feedback was positive.

Though the thought of doing it again caused me angst; I had a glimpse of what it felt like to be successful.

But shortly after, an incident in the same Year 9 class knocked my confidence once again. A notorious bully who didn't enjoy losing her debate against my team targeted me in a peer assessment exercise. In front of the entire class, she belittled me and made fun of what I'd said. Her words felt like the stab and twist of a knife, and everyone laughed at me. For the rest of the year, I remained quiet in class. I believed I didn't deserve to be heard.

The following year, much to my surprise, the deputy principal asked me to join the school debating team. While I felt small moments of success, my teammates seemed superb at thinking on their feet and making the audience sit forward to listen intently. I wanted to be like them. I admired their skills in impromptu speaking, but I didn't believe I could do it. I wasted so much time listening to my fears that I couldn't focus on success.

In Year 12, again to my immense surprise, I was encouraged to enter the Lions Youth of the Year contest, which put my impromptu speaking and presentation skills to the test. It terrified me. I prepared my speech and practised it over and over again and had a good feeling about it. On the day of the contest, I decided I couldn't do it and failed dismally at the impromptu section. For the prepared presentation I had a different attitude. I was presenting on a topic I was passionate about; opportunities for women in leadership positions. My speech was thoroughly researched, and I had plenty to say. Naively I hadn't considered whether my speech would resonate with a room full of male Lions Club members.

My story

Terror gripped me as I walked onto the stage, a feeling that was second nature to me. Stumbling over the first few words, I soon settled in and spoke with confidence, energy and passion. The audience were on the edge of their seats listening, nodding, smiling and appreciating, and I loved it. At the end of my presentation, I received a standing ovation. It was exhilarating to be heard and experience what it felt like to believe in myself.

After leaving school and qualifying as a teacher, I spent eight years teaching drama and English. I communicated effectively and empowered many of my students to be heard. My job was enjoyable, but I wasn't passionate about it, so I pursued other career interests.

A few years ago, whilst working in the public service, I attended a meeting where I planned to give a presentation about a project I'd managed. I was keen to share the findings. Before the meeting, a senior manager told me to give him my project report. He instructed me not to speak in the meeting, implying I wasn't high enough in the hierarchy to be heard. When the manager introduced me, he understated my role and status on the project. Questions were asked that couldn't be answered by anyone else, but I wasn't given the opportunity to speak. Others took the credit for my work, and I left feeling devalued and deflated. This experience finally gave me the impetus to take control of my fears and self-doubt. I realised I had a hunger to be heard.

But I needed support to achieve this change.

This led to one of the most empowering decisions of my life. In 2013, I joined Toastmasters International, a public speaking and leadership organisation. I was exactly where I needed to be. From the beginning, supportive people encouraged me to develop my skills so I could become a quality communicator who believed in herself ... and it really worked. In my first meeting, I noticed the words on the Toastmaster banner which spoke to me intimately: 'Feel the fear and do it anyway'.

My first speech, my icebreaker, was an opportunity to introduce myself. I spoke about my past public speaking experiences, comparing them to a roller coaster ride. I recalled experiencing anticipation, anxiety, nerves, and fear as the cable car climbed the steep slope and then a tremendous feeling of exhilaration and self-satisfaction during the descent to the conclusion of the ride.

My Toastmasters icebreaker made me feel the same way. I compared myself to all of those well-practised speakers and felt fearful about them judging my performance. I rehearsed my speech to death and felt physically sick during the evening leading up to my presentation. When I began speaking, my hands were sweaty, my throat was dry and my heart was pumping so hard I thought it would explode through my chest, much like the fear of ascending a roller coaster track. But once I was about a third of the way through my speech, I felt the audience's support, and I started to enjoy it. The feedback received helped me recognise I already had some sound skills and could become a more powerful presenter.

My involvement in Toastmasters changed everything. I was thriving. Presenting and impromptu speaking became my passion, and I quickly gained a reputation for providing invaluable coaching and feedback to others. I began winning public speaking contests, and in 2015, I competed in Launceston, Tasmania, against interstate Toastmaster peers. It was exhilarating to have had the opportunity to present in front of such a large audience and at such a prestigious event. But at the same time, those feelings of fear and self-doubt crept back. I questioned whether

My story

I was good enough. I acknowledged my fear but decided I was in control; I had the power to enjoy and embrace this opportunity.

My first public speaking experience as a five-year-old was vivid in my mind. When my name was announced to approach the stage, my five-year-old self grabbed my hand, and we practically skipped onto the stage together with excitement. This time I looked around at the sea of faces and smiled, and they smiled back. I presented with ease. I won first prize and was announced as Evaluation District Champion for my abilities to provide feedback and coaching to others. I felt elated, proud and amazed at my achievement. It was time to let go of my old negative memory. My determination to conquer my fears and be willing to go outside my comfort zone time and time again was paying off. Finally, I knew deep down I could be my best self when communicating. I could speak with confidence.

Now I can honestly say I enjoy it, and so can you.

Soon after the contest, I began working with a life and business coach. Together, we discussed my career path, my strengths, and my passions. We identified my yearning to share what I'd learnt, to be heard by others, and to help those who'd experienced similar feelings of fear and self-doubt. My coach encouraged me to start my own business. He told me that my story and my strengths were being wasted by not coaching others to conquer their fears to become powerful communicators. Of course, my first reaction was to think of all the reasons I shouldn't do it, but it was fear talking. I told fear to keep quiet and began building my business, which made me so happy.

Now I make a difference in the lives of others who need my help to realise that fear doesn't need to hold them back. I love making a difference, and I am successful at it because I really get you and your struggles.

In this book, I share what I've learnt over the years by taking myself out of my comfort zone and being dedicated to improving and changing. You, too, can conquer your fears, find your confident voice, follow your passion, and thrive. You, like me, deserve to be heard.

Part I
Understanding your fear

1 YOU CAN OVERCOME FEAR AND SELF-DOUBT

Every day I work with clients who describe the trepidation and anxiety they feel each time they need to speak in public. And we're not talking about standing alone on a stage with a microphone in front of a thousand people. We're talking about common, everyday situations – like contributing an idea during a meeting, giving a work presentation, talking to a small panel in a job interview, giving a speech at a wedding or even chatting with new people at a networking or social get-together.

You are not alone

If you've picked up this book, chances are you're feeling that same fear. And it's not surprising. The National Social Anxiety Centre in the United States reported in a blog in 2017 that:

> The fear of public speaking is the most common phobia ahead of death, spiders, or heights. The National Institute of Mental Health reports that public speaking anxiety ... affects about 73% of the population. The underlying fear is judgment or negative evaluation of others. (Montopoli 2017)

You're not the only one who fears public speaking. It's so common in our society that it has a name: glossophobia.

The trouble is, if you fear public speaking, you probably avoid it as much as possible. And avoiding the thing you fear can lead to problems.

The first problem is that avoiding something because you fear it actually feeds the fear. It puts fear in control and allows it to grow and to cement as a habit.

The second and most significant problem is that by avoiding speaking up, you'll never be heard.

And you deserve to be heard.

You deserve the opportunity to progress in your career, in your interests and in life. You deserve the opportunity to put your ideas forward with confidence and clarity. To make your unique contribution. To state your feelings or your point of view with confidence, and to listen and react to others' points of view.

When you stop to think about it, your fear of speaking in public is really just a bad habit. And like all bad habits, it can be broken. We can break it together.

But first, we need to look at why we torture ourselves with the fear of public speaking so we can better understand it. To do this, we'll break it down and tackle it simply and safely.

It's time to regain your power and find your voice.

Why you suffer from self-criticism and self-doubt

While some of us experience mild anxiety when we need to speak in public, others find it so debilitating they avoid it at all costs. Whether your fear is mild or strong, it's holding you back, so it's worth exploring where it's coming from.

You can overcome fear and self-doubt

Clients tell me that when they imagine themselves speaking in public, they fear:

- embarrassing or humiliating themselves
- not knowing how to handle unknown or unforeseen circumstances
- their audience not being interested in what they have to say
- their audience being critical because they've heard it all before
- not being good enough for people to want to hear what they have to say (imposter syndrome)
- failing completely in front of others.

Can you remember a time when you communicated and received negative feedback? Perhaps you were ignored or misunderstood, or maybe the way you spoke was criticised. You may now think you have nothing unique or worthwhile to share. The experience likely led to you questioning your value or credibility. It's also probable you still feel terrified at the prospect of speaking in front of others. You may be sitting on a particular memory of a time where you felt you failed, and perhaps you've held on to this moment all your life as an excuse to avoid being heard.

In her book *Big Magic*, Elizabeth Gilbert (2016), the bestselling author of *Eat Pray Love*, examines how we often let fear control us because we're 'afraid of being rejected or criticised or ridiculed or misunderstood or worst of all ignored'. She explains that fear needs to be acknowledged; it plays an important part in our survival and our 'fight or flight' response. But we need to take control of fear, so it doesn't hold us back from being creative, innovative, doing the things we love and expressing what matters to us.

Facing your fear

Have you ever wondered what's happening to your body when you experience intense fear or nerves? You may recognise some of the common symptoms: your heart beating faster, sweating, shaking, feeling faint or nauseous.

It may surprise you to know that being a bit nervous is a positive thing. It causes an increased adrenaline flow, and extra blood and oxygen rushes to the muscles and brain. The positive part is it assists you in presenting with more energy and presence. When your nerves escalate to fear, and you allow it to take control, when you waste your energy imagining all the terrible things that could happen, you risk losing focus and the ability to think clearly about what you want to say. This is why many people report having a mental blank or their brain freezing up on them. When you fear your brain freezing, your anxiety increases and makes it more likely that your brain really will freeze! You're channelling your energy in the wrong way by letting fear take a front seat, by letting it take the reins instead of acknowledging it and taking back control. Elizabeth Gilbert encourages you to 'have the courage to bring forth the treasures that are hidden within you …' If you're able to share your thoughts with courage, confidence and clarity, others are more likely to hear you.

You can overcome fear and self-doubt

CLIENT STORY: She faced her fears

A couple of years ago, I facilitated a leadership workshop with a group of young women. As I began, I asked them to describe how they feel when they speak in public. One participant stood out – she explained it made her feel sick and like fainting. By the look on her face, I could tell that was how she felt at that very moment.

A major part of the workshop was to identify and work toward controlling fear. I provided easy tools and strategies they could use leading up to and during their presentation to help them feel more confident and equipped to face their fears. I reassured them they were not alone in their fear, but if they were willing to put themselves outside their comfort zone, in this safe learning environment, they would succeed. Participants then worked in groups to develop short pitches (presentations for ideas and issues they were passionate about).

We had time for volunteers to present their pitches. At first, there was silence. I urged the group to take advantage of this opportunity to try facing their fears. To my surprise, the first volunteer was the young woman who'd stood out at the beginning of the workshop and expressed her intense fear at the thought of public speaking. She walked up the front with a confident stride, stood and faced the audience and spoke with passion and energy. It was raw, emotional, and at the end, she was beaming because she sensed she'd not only succeeded in being heard but had proudly faced her fears. She'd taken her fear with her, decided where it would sit, and took control of it. She was a perfect example of someone who had the 'courage to bring forth the treasures hidden within her'. Her ideas, passions and desire to make a difference as a leader were the treasures. She spoke proudly, because she didn't let fear take over.

She realised she deserved to be heard.

Your past doesn't have to dictate your future

Just like me, you've probably had public speaking experiences that make you cringe. But your past public speaking experiences need not dictate your future. If you're determined to break your cycle of fear, you can. If you're willing to take risks and try new things, it will become easier each time you do it.

It's like learning any new skill, learning to ride a bike, for instance. In the beginning, you feel a bit wobbly. With some practice, and better still with a caring teacher who gives you tips that build your confidence, you will be off your training wheels in no time. You may fall off a few times along the way, but if you're willing to 'get back on the bike', you'll master this new skill. It's the same with public speaking. If you're prepared to persevere, to 'feel the fear and do it anyway' and ride through the wobbly times, you'll find your confidence. You will be heard.

Simon Sinek, thought leader, presenter and author of *Start With Why: How Great Leaders Inspire Everyone To Take Action* (2011), suggests in his YouTube video *Nervous vs Excited* (2018) that we have the power to rewrite our narrative, so we have a different attitude in circumstances where we feel nervous. He describes the example of how he feels nervous when he flies in airplanes, but since he's changed the language, he now tells himself to feel excited, not anxious, and this has changed his reality.

He uses the same strategy when he undertakes major public speaking presentations. He tells himself, 'This is so exciting; I have an opportunity to talk to a group of people who can actually effect change in this country'. If you can use the language of excitement instead of fear or nerves, this will help you to change your attitude and how you feel.

You can overcome fear and self-doubt

This strategy will work especially well if you can explain the reasons for your excitement just like Sinek did about his public speaking.

Facing your fear of speaking is a courageous decision. You should aim to create more positive memories and experiences by taking every opportunity to speak and change the language you use when you talk about it. But don't put pressure on yourself and expect to be perfect every time. Prepare to the best of your ability and be satisfied with results that are sometimes far from perfect. It doesn't matter! You'll slowly change your reality by giving yourself the opportunity to experience success. Be willing to do things that are uncomfortable; little by little, you'll break your cycle of fear.

> *You have the power to change by acknowledging and facing your fear.*

2 MANAGING YOUR FEAR

The next time fear challenges you; I encourage you to feel the fear, but don't let it defeat you. These easy-to-apply tips have helped many of my clients, and they'll help you too.

Diaphragm breathing

When we feel scared, we tend to breathe from our upper chest involuntarily. Breathing like this encourages short, shallow breaths that can increase our feelings of fear. Upper chest breathing can make you look and feel nervous.

Upper chest breathing also makes it obvious to your audience that you're feeling scared or nervous. They may notice visible symptoms such as holding your shoulders and neck rigidly and that you sound breathy. This not only makes you *look* less confident but also makes you *feel* more uptight and nervous. The more relaxed you can appear, the more relaxed your audience will be, and the more likely it is they'll hear what you have to say clearly. On the other hand, if you're obviously nervous, your audience may find themselves distracted; they'll likely focus on your nerves and feel nervous for you.

When I coach clients who feel fearful about public speaking, I always begin with diaphragm breathing. This eases anxiety and helps us to feel and sound better. It also has the physiological benefits of slowing the heart rate and has a calming effect.

 Tip #1 Use diaphragm breathing to ease your nerves

Diaphragm breathing is powerful. It means dropping your breath from your upper chest down to your belly. If you have trouble achieving diaphragm breathing, try these methods:

Method 1

When you're practising at home, lie on your back and place a book on your belly. The aim of this is to direct your attention to that area of your body while watching and feeling the book rise and fall. Once you've mastered this lying down, progress your practice while standing and in a seated position.

Method 2

Activate your core muscles by gently pulling in your navel (like you'd do in pilates). This will help the brain to focus on that area. When you release your belly button, breathe out and repeat.

You may have already learnt breathing methods that help you calm your nerves. I encourage you to use any method that works for you. One of my favourites is holding my palms face up and slowly folding my fingers in as I breathe in, uncurling my fingers as I breathe out. This is a useful tool for calming the nervous system as it ignites the senses of touch and sight. You can also hold your hands under a desk at a meeting or interview if you're feeling anxious. Nobody will know what you're doing!

However, for addressing anxiety while speaking, diaphragm breathing is your best tool. It helps with nerves and improves vocal quality by removing breathiness, supporting voice projection and assisting you to avoid speaking too quickly.

> *It's important to use diaphragm breathing well before you're in a situation when you may feel nervous.*

On the day of a presentation or interview, begin diaphragm breathing when you wake up – you'll start the day by reminding yourself of its importance and feel more relaxed and focussed. Don't wait until you're feeling anxious because then it may be too late.

You can use diaphragm breathing up until and even during your presentation. It's crucial to pause and breathe at those moments when you may lose your place or when asked a difficult question.

To access my 'Nine-step breathing method for calming your nerves on the day of your presentation', visit this link on my website: www.completecommunicationcoach.com.au/YDTBH

Many clients have had success using this method:

'Kerry gave me the confidence to go in there and smash my interview yesterday. I remembered to breathe, pause, speak slowly, and have faith in myself.' (**Kathryn, public servant, 2019**)

'Fears and nerves used to cause me so much stress before presenting, so it's great to be able to just focus on presenting rather than worrying about things going wrong.' (**Youth volunteer, Headspace, 2018**)

'I will use the breathing from the diaphragm technique; it will be great for nerve release – very important for when things feel stressful or scary.' (**Year 12 school leader, 2020**)

Body language matters

Your body language is noticed before your words. You influence how your audience perceives you by the way you sit, stand and walk.

 Tip #2 Pause before you begin speaking

I vividly recall a workshop I attended with Dananjaya Hettiarachchi, the 2014 Toastmasters International World Champion of Public Speaking. He commented, you shouldn't begin speaking as soon as you face your audience. If you do, the audience won't clearly hear and digest the first few words you say. It may not seem natural to you at first, but pausing before you speak will give your audience time to connect with you.

Building trust and influence

When you use body language effectively, you put yourself in a strong position to build rapport and trust. This makes the difference between successfully engaging with and influencing your audience, or not.

If your body language is ineffective, you'll look unconfident or disinterested. You can confuse, distract or even offend your audience, and this creates barriers to being heard. I often observe people using distracting body language by putting their hands in pockets, hand clasping, looking at the ceiling or floor, pacing, folding arms or legs and fidgeting.

This leads me to a powerful story of a person who attended one of my workshops.

CLIENT STORY: He stood tall and found his voice

A participant in one of my group workshops demonstrated the impact body language can have on how we look and feel. His shoulders were rounded, and he avoided eye contact. The questions he asked during the workshop demonstrated his fear of letting himself go, taking a risk and getting up in front of an audience. When I spoke about gesturing, he commented he felt more comfortable with his hands behind his back. He said this was more natural to him, that gesturing would make his mind go blank. I explained I was offering a range of tools, some of which may suit some people more than others. We all have our own authentic communication style. He seemed unconvinced.

When the time came for participants to share their stories on stage, I invited him to share a story about what was important to him. What followed was one of the most rewarding moments of my career. This young man, who'd spent the day cowering in his seat in fear, stood up – TALL – with his shoulders back and walked to the stage with sheer determination. I hadn't even noticed how tall he was because his body language when seated was so closed.

He reached the stage, stood in a power pose, looked around the room, made confident and inclusive eye contact and shared one of the most emotive and powerful personal stories I'd ever heard. At the end of the story, the audience applauded loudly. He smiled (for the first time that day) and turned to me, saying, 'I want to share my story to huge audiences of hundreds of people so I can help others who have gone through what I've been through.'

I watched him physically and emotionally grow as he connected powerfully with his audience. I think of this moment still; it remains a wonderful example of how body language can greatly impact you and others.

Looking and feeling more confident

Be mindful of your body language and how you and your audience may interpret it.

Amy Cuddy, social psychologist, discusses her research (2015) in her TED Talk *Your Body Language May Shape Who You Are*, describing how open body language makes you look and feel more confident. Open body language means taking up as much space as possible, spreading out, standing tall with your shoulders back and head up, together with a wide smile and confident eye contact. These strategies will make you appear confident, regardless of how you feel inside. If you make yourself smaller by crossing your arms or legs, rounding your shoulders, touching your face or avoiding eye contact, you'll seem unconfident, untrustworthy or unsure of yourself.

Cuddy researched body language used in job interviews and concluded that those who appeared confident were much more likely to be hired than those who looked stressed or uncertain – regardless of what they actually had to say.

 **Tip #3** Use open body language

Not only will you look more confident with open body language, but you'll also feel more confident and powerful. Your actions will influence your thoughts and feelings. Do you recall seeing cartoon images of Wonder Woman and Superman? You'd never catch them folding their arms, crossing their legs or looking unconfident and not in control. They stand tall, with their shoulders back and down, head up, hands on hips, legs hip-width apart and evenly weighted on the floor.

Cuddy refers to this as *power posing*. She suggests if you hold a power pose for up to two minutes, you'll influence your brain, and you'll start to feel like a superhero too.

Another form of power pose is to throw your arms up into a V sign in the air whilst standing tall. Cuddy shared stories of blind athletes who had never seen body language that symbolises victory and power. After major running events, they instinctively run over the finish line, throwing their arms in the air in a victory sign because it feels naturally powerful.

Whenever I'm about to enter the stage for a public speaking contest or take part in an interview, or even when I'm about to meet a new client, I do a power pose beforehand. I'm not suggesting that when you face an audience at a presentation, at a meeting or a job interview, you stand in a power pose. Your audience might look at you strangely if you do.

Before you enter a situation and if you're feeling nervous or unsure of yourself, find a private place to practice power posing. This could be in the car park, the toilets or a meeting room. Just before you enter the space, drop your hands from your hips to your sides, whilst maintaining your strong and confident posture. I've taught this technique in many workshops with consistent success. If you'd like to access a cheat sheet where I describe how to achieve this in eight easy steps, please visit my website via this link: www.completecommunicationcoach.com.au/YDTBH

Managing your fear

Power Posing: Joanne Kneebone and Kerry Pienaar

> "It works for Wonder Woman, it works for me, and it can work for you too!"

Expect success

There are many tools you can use to set yourself up for success. If you do some preparation for a presentation or job interview, for example, you're likely to tackle these challenges with a positive attitude, which increases your chances of success.

If you assume you're going to have a negative experience, it's much more likely you will. Often when we feel nervous and experience self-doubt, we find ourselves imagining all the things that could go wrong.

- What if I forget my lines?
- What if I have a mental blank?
- What if the audience doesn't like me?
- What if I drop my notes?
- What if I don't understand an interview question?

And the list can go on if you let it.

Tip #4 Identify and troubleshoot your what-ifs in advance

Rather than panic about the what-ifs in the moment, troubleshoot answers before the event.

Managing your fear

> **Example 1:** *What if* the audience has blank faces?
>
> **Answer:** There's often at least one friendly face in the audience. If this isn't the case for you, try to connect with someone at the event before it's your turn to speak. Notice where they're sitting and when you enter the stage, make eye contact and smile at them. If you know them well, you could ask them to smile at you first to give you a positive start and make it easier for you to smile back naturally. In most cases, people are in the audience because they want to hear from you. They want you to succeed. If there are one or two people in the audience who don't appear to be supportive, don't give them your attention. Focus on those who are interested and engaged.

> **Example 2:** *What if* I lose my place or have a mental blank?
>
> **Answer:** Remember, your audience is probably hearing what you have to say for the first time. If you miss a section or forget what comes next, they won't know! Don't apologise, don't panic. Just pause and breathe from your diaphragm while you give yourself time to think and find your place. Pausing is incredibly valuable. It allows your audience time to think and digest what you've said. It adds impact. Pausing also helps you to collect yourself, whereas panicking makes it hard to find your place. If you're well prepared, have rehearsed what you want to say and organised your presentation in a logical sequence, it'll be easier to collect your thoughts and find your place.

> **Example 3:** *What if* I don't understand an interview question?
>
> **Answer:** If you don't understand a question when you first hear it, don't panic. If you're finding a question hard, it's likely others also may be stumped. Pause and breathe so you can think clearly. Don't make the mistake of pretending you know the answer. Ask the interviewer to rephrase the question. If you can answer part of the question, do so. If you have no idea, ask if you can come back to that question. While you don't know the answer, you can suggest ways you might go about finding out.

 Tip #5 Anticipate and expect success when you communicate

We all learn in different ways. If you're a visual learner, you can **use visualisation exercises** to imagine success leading up to an event. Each day, for seven days before an event such as a job interview, a meeting, a networking occasion, a work presentation or a speech at a wedding, close your eyes and picture how you want it to turn out.

> **Visualising success for a networking event**
>
> Picture yourself walking into a networking event with strong and open body language. Confidently scan the room to decide who you'd like to approach. Walk up to a group, smile and make eye contact. Begin introducing yourself and making conversation with ease. Notice the body language of the people you're speaking with. They smile and nod as you speak and lean forward with keen interest. You really enjoy the experience; in fact, it's lots of fun meeting new people and sharing your story.

If you have trouble visualising, you may prefer to write about your success. Reading what you've written may have more impact on you. Each day, for seven days before an event, describe your ideal scenario in writing.

> **Writing about success for a job interview**
>
> I arrive at my job interview brimming with confidence, telling myself the interviewers will quickly recognise this job has been designed specifically for me. I allow plenty of time to do some diaphragmatic breathing to keep me centred and calm. I look at myself in the mirror in the bathroom while I practice a power pose. My posture is confident, and I smile because I'm looking forward to finding out more about the position. I stand and wait calmly in the waiting room. The chairperson of the panel approaches me. I look them directly in the eye and smile while introducing myself, creating a positive first impression. The chairperson introduces me to the interviewers who smile and make me feel comfortable and welcome. I'm asked the first question, which I answer easily. As the interview progresses, I gain confidence. My interviewers are nodding and smiling; they can clearly see I have the credentials, skills and strengths for this position. This is the best job interview I've ever done.

If you're an aural learner, you could audio record how you want a situation to play out or **say it aloud** in a quiet space each day for a week leading up to the event. For example, try reciting your wedding speech in the shower or the car as you drive.

> ### Speaking aloud about success for a wedding speech
>
> I arrive at the wedding reception and check where the speeches will occur. I begin deep breathing to keep myself calm and centred. I sit, feeling relaxed, enjoy my entrée and make enjoyable conversation with the people at my table. I'm introduced to the audience and receive raucous applause and smiles as I stand and walk with authority to the stage. I pause to take in the sea of smiling faces, smile back and make eye contact. I feel an immediate connection with the audience. They laugh loudly at my first joke, which gives me confidence. I can sense they're moved and show obvious appreciation of the heartfelt stories I share about my dear friends. At one point, I get caught up in the emotion and lose my place, but I recover quickly by pausing, smiling, and breathing. There is thunderous applause at the end of the presentation, and I walk off with great satisfaction. It was so much fun and such an honour. I wish I could do it again.

Get out of your comfort zone

When we fear something, we often avoid it at all costs. Many of the people I meet have spent a lifetime terrified of public speaking and use every excuse to avoid it. Not speaking in public can seriously impact our lives. For example, it creates a barrier to career advancement. Many jobs require us to have the ability and confidence to give presentations and to communicate with authority and influence.

Tip #6 Be prepared to face your fear to gain experience and build confidence

It's incredibly satisfying to help my clients turn their careers around. Often a big part of this is by encouraging them to challenge their fears head-on. The starting point is always deciding to make a change. Chip away at it in baby steps if you need to, or take a giant leap to accelerate your progress. If you volunteer for public speaking assignments, are prepared to speak in a meeting, and practice the tools and strategies I discuss, you'll find each time it becomes easier, and you become a little less fearful. I refer to this as 'getting out of your comfort zone'. It's essentially deciding you want to change, being specific about how and when you'll do it, and then practicing whenever you get the chance. Eventually, you may actually enjoy the exhilaration of public speaking success.

CLIENT STORY: Facing her fears was transformative

A client came to me recently who I'll call 'Jill' to preserve her privacy.

Jill had just recently started a new job which she was very excited about but terrified at the same time because she knew it was finally time to face her fears. She learnt she'd have to undertake public speaking as a critical part of her role. Previously she'd avoided public speaking at all costs, as it made her feel physically sick and caused her to lose sleep. She contacted me because she was finally ready to face her fears and no longer let them hold her back. As a coach, it was incredibly rewarding to help this young woman shine.

'With Kerry's guidance, I went from struggling to speak at team meetings to delivering a polished presentation to forty staff in a government department. Kerry provided me with strategies that empowered me to take a leap of faith and face my fears head-on. She also provided a safe space to practice my presentations and provided constructive feedback in a friendly way. The skills I've learned from Kerry have been transformative for both my confidence and my career. I experienced huge changes in just two sessions with Kerry, and I would not hesitate to recommend her services to anyone who wants to improve their public speaking skills.' ('Jill', researcher, 2021)

> *The more you take yourself out of your comfort zone, the more confident you will become.*

Summary of tips for managing your fears

Tip #1 Use diaphragm breathing to ease nerves.

Tip #2 Pause before you begin speaking.

Tip #3 Use open body language.

Tip #4 Identify and troubleshoot your what-ifs in advance.

Tip #5 Anticipate and expect success when you communicate.

Tip #6 Be prepared to face your fears to gain experience and build confidence.

Part II
Taking control

3 CREATE CONNECTIONS AND BUILD TRUST

If you want to be heard, a critical starting point is to create connections with your audience, whether your audience is small or large. But what's the best way to do this?

This chapter looks at the art of building a connection and the neuroscience and psychology behind it. It's important to understand a little of the science behind human interaction, so you can effectively engage, influence, inspire and build trust with audiences.

Dr Fiona Kerr, Industry Professor at the University of Adelaide, is an expert in the field of neuroscience and human connectivity. In her TEDx Talk *How leaders change brains and win hearts* (2017), she discusses her 2013 research explaining we are 'hardwired to connect'. Face-to-face communication builds trust neurons in the brain, which help you to build a relationship immediately – within one twentieth of a second of meeting someone. If your audience trust you and feel supported, they are more likely to take the time to listen to you, to take action and to understand what you have to say. This can have a profound influence on your success as a communicator and as a leader. It causes a range of neural activity to occur for you and your audience, whether you're giving a presentation or communicating in a meeting. This may include spindle neurons, mirror neurons, oxytocin, and dopamine. Together these contribute to changing the behaviour of the brain and impact on the relationships you build. Trusting relationships are your key to influence.

Eye contact

One of the most effective ways to connect with your audience and build trust is to make eye contact. Ironically, many of us avoid this as it makes us feel uncomfortable. If you avoid eye contact, you could appear unsure of yourself or even untrustworthy.

Tip #7 Maintain eye contact

Dr Fiona Kerr collaborated to undertake some fascinating research into how we connect through eye contact (Kerr F, et al 2016). She discusses this research in her Tedx Talk *Look Into My Eyes* (2016), explaining that 'when we first start to lock eyes with a person … we start creating a connection'. When you look deeply into someone's eyes, and they return the favour, you create a retinal eye lock. Dr Kerr says, 'One of your retinas aligns with one of their retinas. This causes the right hemisphere of your brain to synchronise with the right hemisphere of their brain.' Retinal connection supports creativity, promotes better collaboration, and helps develop empathy, all of which assist your audience to feel connected and valued. When they feel this way, they're more likely to listen attentively and respectfully.

If you want to develop trust, to influence or to calm someone – look directly at them. This can be an effective strategy whether you're trying to sell something as a salesperson, share an idea in a meeting, or convince an interviewer of your skills. If your audience is initially feeling nervous or uncertain about you or your idea, you have the power and influence to change their minds, and to calm them.

Create connections and build trust

Effective eye contact helps you engage and maintain connection with any size audience, show sincerity and gauge how others feel. Even when you're introduced as a presenter, make eye contact with audience members as you walk to the stage to build immediate connection. Use inclusive eye contact when you're communicating with a group: avoid the common mistake of focussing on just one or two people.

When you make eye contact, it's important to keep your audience's comfort in mind. Here are some guidelines to consider. If your eye contact is:

- **too short,** your eyes appear to dart quickly from one person to the next; this can make you look nervous
- **too long,** you encroach on the personal space and comfort of an audience member, and potentially make yourself seem over-intense or unsociable
- **too predictable,** that is, looking from side to side rhythmically, can make it seem as if you're watching a tennis match. This can distract the audience from listening to you.

Dr Kerr suggests that if you're not talking directly to someone or if you become distracted, you risk disconnecting from your audience. This may result in them coming up with reasons they shouldn't listen to you or believe what you're saying. It's known as 'disconfirming behaviour'. For example, avoid the distracting habit of looking up or down as you're thinking. This interrupts your connection, and you could even find the audience looking to see what's on the ceiling or floor.

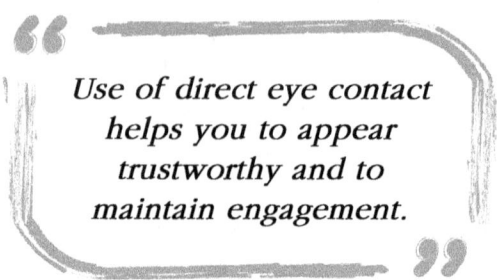

> *Use of direct eye contact helps you to appear trustworthy and to maintain engagement.*

Be aware of cultural sensitivities around body language, such as eye contact and gestures, so you don't offend or create misunderstanding or misinterpretation. This may require some research on your part and the need to tailor your body language for different audiences. For example, people from some cultures may not feel comfortable using direct eye contact, and hand gestures can be colloquial.

Smiling is contagious

Smiling seems so simple, yet it makes such a difference. If you smile at someone, they're likely to smile back. And we know how good this makes us feel. The effects are the same whether we have an audience of one or one hundred. We remember people who smile.

 Tip #8 Smile at your audience

Ding Li (2014), winner of the Young Science Communicator's Competition (YSCC) and one of the world's most talented young communicators, is particularly interested in the benefits of smiling and how it helps us to connect. Feeling happy stimulates the release of endorphins and sends signals to our facial muscles, resulting in a smile. Smiling helps to reduce anxiety. It lowers

Create connections and build trust

blood pressure and our heart rate, so it's a valuable tool for putting both you and your audience at ease.

If smiling doesn't come naturally to you, you can fake it! The benefits are the same. The key is to make sure that when you smile, it's deep enough to create creases around your eyes (and not just your mouth). Smiling with an open mouth looks more authentic. Smiling while you're talking helps too. It impacts the tone of your voice and consequently influences the way your audience perceives you.

Smiling is contagious whenever and wherever you communicate. When you meet someone, often first impressions are influenced by a smile. Imagine if you're the only candidate to smile at a job interview or the only barista to smile at your customers, the only manager who smiles at their team or the only salesperson who smiles at a potential customer. You will stand out. You'll be more likely to be trusted, to build relationships, to influence, to be remembered and to be heard. You'll stand out because you built a connection, and in doing so, you're helping your audience to listen and trust you.

In my early days speaking at Toastmasters, I felt incredibly nervous. I'd concentrate hard to remember what I wanted to share at the expense of connecting, which left me appearing intense and serious. The feedback given seemed so simple, yet had an enormous impact. They advised me to smile at my audience. That was it. They assured me it would make me feel happier and less anxious, and in turn, my audience would relax, too.

It was also suggested that before speaking, I should pause, breathe and choose a friend in the audience (or someone I felt comfortable with), and smile directly at them. I made a point of teeing this up with someone in the audience before each of my presentations. I would ask them to smile at me to make it easier for me to smile back when I most needed it.

I discovered the benefits of smiling. It now comes naturally to me, but it took practice.

Don't forget to smile – even on the phone. The difference in your voice can be heard, and your listener is more likely to feel at ease. The more relaxed you and your audience are, the easier it is for them to listen actively to you.

Gesture to influence

Vanessa Van Edwards (2017) researched what made certain TED Talks more successful than others. She found something surprising – it was the presenters who used the most gestures that went viral. These presenters not only knew how to share their ideas verbally, but they could explain and support them with their gestures. Van Edwards suggests audiences notice hand movements before almost anything else when it comes to body language.

Gestures can help you describe or emphasise a point. They should match and support what you're saying (except where you're using gestures to be humorous, of course). Be as natural as possible when you gesture because the audience will notice if you force them, and it won't look authentic.

Tip #9 Use open palm gestures

Create connections and build trust

Open palm gestures are welcoming and invite your audience to enter your world and share your story.

Have your hands to your sides when you're not gesturing; this allows you to use a full range of gestures easily and purposefully with energy and passion. For presentations in large venues, use larger gestures; include some with straight arms that are raised higher so that those in the back row can see you.

> *Use larger gestures with larger audiences and remember to show your palms.*

A common gesture you should avoid is clasping your hands in front of you. This creates a barrier between you and your audience and can appear protective or closed. It can also give the impression that you're nervous, or don't want to be there. Also, remember your range of movement will be limited if you constantly have your elbows bent or locked at your ribs or if you only gesture from your elbows to your fingertips.

Gesturing too regularly or too intensely or using the same gestures repeatedly can be distracting. For example, I've seen speakers use a distracting gesture known as 'the window wiper' where they sweep their hands backwards and forwards with elbows bent and tucked into their ribs. Others put their hands in their pockets or play with their hair or jewellery, or repeatedly pull at a piece of clothing. Habitually placing your hands behind your back risks making you look unfriendly or even military-like. It can also distract your audience as they wonder what you're hiding behind your back. Audiences feel more comfortable if they can see your hands (though it can also be a mistake to show the audience too much of the back of your hands).

Distracting gestures can result in the audience subconsciously focussing on your actions rather than your words. Gestures should support your words, not overtake them.

 Tip #10 Avoid gestures that distract

It's a useful strategy to ask a friend to observe you when you're presenting (or even just in conversation). Ask them to give you feedback about how and when you gesture and how effective it is. Once you have this knowledge, you can build on it.

You could even video record your presentation and observe how you look. If you'd like some extra help to get started and would like access to a cheat sheet on some gestures to try, visit this link: www.completecommunicationcoach.com.au/YDTBH

Read the room

When you're presenting or participating in a meeting or interview, most audiences (apart from the occasional exception) will be interested in what you have to say. There's a range of non-verbal cues that can help you know whether your audience is interested, and you can adjust your approach if you need to.

 Tip #11 Tune in to the suite of non-verbal cues

Look for positive non-verbal cues such as nodding, smiling or leaning forward. These show genuine interest and support for what you're saying. If you notice an audience member tilting their head to the side slightly, you know they're completely absorbed in your story.

Be careful not to misinterpret your audience. For example, someone who closes their eyes may not be asleep – they may be concentrating on your words and devising a question for you. Someone with their arms crossed may be feeling cold, not defensive. Mouth covering can demonstrate a lack of confidence but can simply be coughing. Tune in to the suite of signals your audience gives you, so you don't misinterpret the engagement you've already created.

It can be a trap to focus your attention on the minority of people in your audience who show negative body language. For example, someone at the back of the room might be checking their phone or laptop or talking to someone else. DO NOT waste your time focussing on them. Focus instead on those who are genuinely connected with you and give them your energy, passion and undivided attention.

When giving a long presentation, you need to be able to read the room by tuning in to the energy levels and concentration of your audience. The audience typically goes through peaks and troughs. You can influence this by designing and structuring a presentation or workshop that responds to the peaks and troughs. For example, after lunch, the audience tends to be fatigued and need your help to build their energy levels. You can do this by providing energiser activities that encourage active participation and facilitates a new peak in their concentration. It is also important to 'change it up' frequently, presenting different formats and a variety of activities especially if presenting for a half or full day. These can include small group discussions, short activities in pairs or use of videos, props or other visual aids. You can also change it up in your presentation delivery by turning off presentation slides, so the audience can shift their focus. Changing the volume, pace and pitch of your voice, and using purposeful movement to engage your audience more directly are also useful tools.

Share stories

Stories are a great way to show your audience why something matters to you. They help people connect with you on an emotional level and leave a lasting impression. If you ask an audience member what they remember about your presentation weeks, months, or even years down the track, your stories will win every time. Through stories, audiences are more likely to empathise and care about you and your message. They'll see that you're genuine and prepared to be open and vulnerable.

Tip #12 Tell stories to evoke emotion

Stories evoke emotions. They make us laugh, cry, get angry and feel inspired. I carefully chose the stories used to illustrate various points in this book as they help bring to life what I'm trying to convey. They are raw, real, and authentic. When you share a story, you paint a picture in your audience's mind, and this can influence them to act.

Bosworth and Zolden (2012) suggest that before scientists could map the neural pathways, it was assumed that influence was based on logic rather than emotion. Presentations often emphasise facts, figures and quotes, which of course are important. However, Neuroscience shows us that the brain produces an emotional response before a logical one: 'We're hardwired to feel first, think second' (Bosworth and Zolden 2012: 22).

Also, Bosworth and Zolden state that 'Memories are formed in the limbic areas, the emotional brain … In the long run, we tend to remember more clearly the way an experience made us feel than the facts and details associated with that experience …' (Bosworth and Zolden 2012: 28).

Use stories along with facts to bring your presentations to life. Use vivid language to describe scenes and characters and include dialogue; all of this evokes the senses and triggers the emotions. You can make your story even more colourful by using devices such as metaphors and analogies.

Bosworth and Zolden (2012) reminds us that we're natural storytellers and story listeners who love learning through narrative. When we're told we're going to hear a story, we relax, focus and pay attention. That's why stories are so effective for young children at bedtime and for adults when presenting, networking, or meeting.

Your stories should be relevant to your message. They should set the scene and ideally include a struggle, challenge or conflict. Most importantly, your story needs to provide a solution, such as the main character experiencing a 'lightbulb moment' that results in a change of perspective or direction. The solution should be tied to the message of your presentation.

> *Stories leave a lasting impression because they evoke emotion and make you memorable.*

The most influential stories are those accompanied by powerful non-verbal communication, such as your tone of voice and body language. These show the strength of the emotion behind your words and bring your story to life.

Create connections and build trust

CLIENT STORY: He showed his vulnerability through a story

A couple of years ago, I ran a training workshop with a group of young volunteers. The focus was on impromptu speaking and storytelling using pre-prepared questions to prompt participants to share their stories.

One volunteer stood out from the rest. He asked if he could share his story about what motivated him to volunteer in this organisation.

He could've just given a factual recount of his motivation to be involved, but instead, he took us on an emotional journey. He described his strong desire to make a difference for others in similar situations. It was one of the most compelling stories I've ever heard.

He described the impact of being bullied all his life because of his sexual preference. He included research and statistics to back up his message, but it was the story that impacted and caused all the audience to be visibly moved. Tears rolled down our cheeks. I can remember that moment so clearly, how it made me feel and what he was trying to achieve by sharing his story. It was raw, authentic, and the speaker connected with all of his audience on an emotional level.

His story motivated others in the room to want to tell their stories, which highlighted his strong leadership qualities. It was one of the most powerful and inspirational moments of my career.

People often tell me they don't have interesting and worthwhile stories to tell. This just isn't true. You'd be amazed at how intrigued people are to hear about your life, your dreams and your experiences. We're all unique and have many worthwhile stories to share.

Think about putting together your own inventory of stories. Start with your childhood. Think of funny things you did, said, saw and experienced. Move onto other funny or embarrassing things that have happened to you. Talk to family members and see what they remember. List stories about people you know who've impacted your life or who you admire. Document experiences that have shaped you, challenged you, or where you believe you've struggled, failed or triumphed.

Tip #13 Create an inventory of stories to share

Having a pre-prepared list of stories to draw upon makes it easier when you're put on the spot or when you're developing a presentation. I'm not suggesting you tell stories for the sake of it, but that you choose a story or two that helps support your message, that paint the picture of what you're trying to convey, communicate or teach. It really works!

You could even create different versions of different lengths for your repertoire of stories to suit varied situations and timeframes. For example, in a job interview, any stories you tell should be short and snappy; however, a sixty-minute keynote presentation at a conference gives you more time to tell an extended story.

Bosworth and Zoldan (2012) suggest story types you can prepare to suit varied scenarios.

Story types (Bosworth and Zoldan 2012)

Who am I?

How you ended up here today.

A story of how you got there with challenges along the way.

The resolution could be what you currently do.

Who do I represent?

A story about your company or business.

The specific story you choose to tell will depend on the point you're trying to make.

The resolution of this story is whatever your business does today that illustrates your message.

Why do I do what I do?

What has led you to your chosen pathway?

What are some of your challenges and triumphs?

What drives you?

Who have I helped?

An example of success stories of people you've worked with, coached, mentored, helped.

What were their challenges, and how did you help them overcome them?

Show passion and authenticity

I've seen people share important information without passion and authenticity. This limits their ability to influence, inspire or move their audience.

If you're telling a story or making a point that means a lot to you, be prepared to show emotion through your voice and body language and really feel what you're sharing. If you use elongated pausing at the end of delivering an emotional point, this will allow the emotion to sink in for your audience.

 Tip #14 Communicate with passion and vulnerability

If you feel excited about what you're sharing, deliver it with enthusiasm and excitement. This will be contagious for your audience and have an uplifting influence. Imagine two people presenting about the same topic. The first has a deadpan face, monotone voice and rigid body. The second uses a full range of descriptive gestures, their face is lit up, and the tone and pitch of their voice is varied. Who's likely to keep your attention?

If you hold yourself back by being fearful of showing your vulnerability, you do yourself and your audience a disservice. Vulnerability is not a sign of weakness, but rather demonstrates courage and creates empathy. It actually makes you stronger in your audience's eyes.

Showing vulnerability can also be contagious and lead to others reciprocating their own vulnerability. Influence others to open up to you, and they're likely to reveal information that you need to identify barriers to their success. According to Bosworth and Zoldan, vulnerability is contagious. 'When people see us opening up and being authentic, they're inclined to open up and be authentic themselves … Allowing yourself to be seen as vulnerable fosters an environment of openness that leads to trust' (Bosworth and Zoldan 2012: 34).

Create connections and build trust

CLIENT STORY: Sisters who exude authenticity and passion

Zia and Cyanne are twin sisters who ensure their voices are heard despite both managing a severe physical disability, limb-girdle muscular dystrophy (LGMD). They have to work harder and rely on others to support them to undertake the basic physical tasks that most of us take for granted. This doesn't stop them from having a voice or wanting to make a difference.

They're inspiring leaders whose voices are heard across their community. Over many years, they've sat on a range of committees and councils increasing awareness and influencing significant improvements for people with disability. Their strong desire to support others has helped to break preconceived stereotypes. They've won awards for their service to the community and have been invited to public speaking engagements where they've shared their stories.

In 2019, they participated in some presentation skills workshops I facilitated. They were unable to stand like the other participants, which limited their use of body language. Nevertheless, Zia and Cyanne were able to connect with the audience through eye contact and smiling and through presenting with sincerity and conviction. They 'read the room' when presenting, through active listening and recognising the body language of others. They made a real connection and left the audience in awe.

Because they voice their passions and exude authenticity, they make audiences sit up and listen. They are immensely inspiring.

I've watched people presenting who seem to be 'putting on an act'. While you might pretend to be confident so your audience doesn't know you're trembling at the knees, you can't pretend to be someone you're not. Audiences can tell if you don't mean what you're saying or if you're not being yourself. Your body language gives you away.

Have you ever compared yourself to your peers when presenting or when communicating in meetings? If you compare yourself to others and try to emulate them, you won't appear authentic. It's important to hold true to your unique strengths and style of delivery.

Tip #15 Be your authentic self

Rehearsing for presentations or job interviews in front of a trusted friend or colleague can help you develop your unique approach. This means making yourself vulnerable. Seeking feedback about your strengths and areas for improvement will help you be a more passionate, influential, and authentic communicator.

If you're reading from a script you don't genuinely believe, it's likely to be obvious to your audience. Over-rehearsed presentations or answers can also affect authenticity and spontaneity. If you're too locked into what you've learnt word for word or rehearsed your gestures too precisely, it can appear unnatural.

When I first joined Toastmasters, I compared myself to others. I was in awe of those who were confident and influential speakers and who won public speaking competitions. The belief I'd never be a great speaker and certainly would never be good enough to enter competitions was strong.

Create connections and build trust

I committed to improving my skills by regularly practising, watching others, and rehearsing and researching the qualities of powerful presenters. There are common strategies we can all use to engage an audience. However, to be authentic, it's important to develop your own unique style while continuing to refine your skills through seeking and acting upon quality feedback.

Being prepared to push myself out of my comfort zone made me a better, more confident and impactful presenter – especially when I spoke about topics I was passionate and knowledgeable about. Before I knew it, I was making people laugh and moving them to tears by telling my stories.

The feedback I consistently receive from my clients is that I'm authentic, and my passion for my work shows. I've become comfortable with revealing my vulnerabilities through sharing stories. My authenticity and passion help my clients to trust me, connect with me, relate to me and take risks to improve.

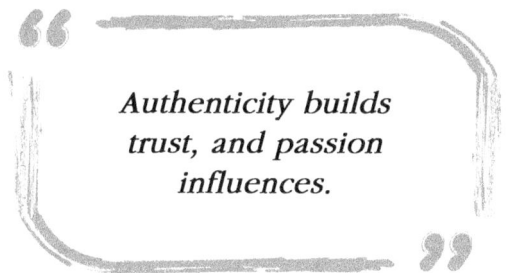

Authenticity builds trust, and passion influences.

Summary of tips for creating connections

Tip #7   Maintain eye contact.

Tip #8   Smile at your audience.

Tip #9   Use open palm gestures.

Tip #10   Avoid gestures that distract.

Tip #11   Tune in to the suite of non-verbal cues.

Tip #12   Tell stories to evoke emotion.

Tip #13   Create an inventory of stories to share.

Tip #14   Communicate with passion and vulnerability.

Tip #15   Be your authentic self.

4 BRING YOUR VOICE TO LIFE

In my previous profession as a drama teacher and through subsequent voice training, I gained many tips and strategies that I share with you in this chapter to help bring your voice to life.

Do people tell you that you speak too quickly, too softly or you don't enunciate clearly? Do you feel your accent may impact the effectiveness of your communication? Have you ever found it hard to remain engaged when listening to someone else speaking?

If you literally can't be heard or understood or you don't have vocal strategies for maintaining your audience's engagement, your problem could be your voice quality. There are strategies for communicating with confidence, clarity, and expression.

Be aware of the 4 Ps: Pitch, Pause, Pace and Projection

We've all been to meetings or presentations where we've struggled to concentrate; often it's because the presenter didn't put into practice 'the 4 Ps'.

Let's look at each of these vocal elements individually. Then we'll explore how they can work together most effectively when you want to keep your audience engaged.

Pitch

Your starting place is to become aware of the pitch range in your speaking voice. While you probably haven't thought much about it, every word you speak has a pitch range – high, medium, or low. Many of us don't change our pitch and may sound repetitive when we're speaking.

Tip #16 Vary the pitch of your voice

Varying pitch makes our vocal pattern less predictable and more interesting to listen to. Many women speak with naturally higher-pitched voices than men, especially when excited. Ask a friend whether you speak in a high-pitched voice. You can then decide whether you want to work at accessing a lower pitch. Aim to identify the middle pitch in your voice and try varying your pitch one level above and one level below when you speak. In a workshop I attended in 2018 with voice coach Marilyn Bodycoat, I acquired some strategies for varying voice pitch.

If you're unsure where your voice is usually pitched, a useful way to experiment is to read aloud from a book. Read a sentence beginning with your lowest pitch level, then read the next sentence at a higher level. Keep going for around five sentences until you reach your highest pitch. If you do this regularly, you'll increase your awareness of pitch when you speak.

Tip #17 Avoid using a rising inflection when not asking a question

An annoying and distracting habit is a rising inflection at the end of a sentence, which in essence means raising your pitch in the wrong place. This distorts communication because it sounds like you're asking a question when you're just making a statement. This can make you sound unsure of yourself or like you're looking for approval. It can also sound like you're talking down to others in a patronising way.

Pause
Pausing is an incredibly powerful communication tool. It helps you to slow down and breathe. It allows time for reflection and helps your audience to digest each piece of information. It adds impact and can even create suspense, drama, anticipation, or emotion.

Remember that although you know your content and thoughts intimately, your audience is hearing it for the first time.

Silence needs to be longer than you think. As a starting point, you can pause at the end of each sentence or section of a presentation.

 **Tip #18** Use purposeful pausing

Pausing is also a useful strategy for avoiding filler words such as 'um', 'err', 'ah' and even 'like', 'I guess', 'you know', and 'what not' … you know the words I mean! These words creep in when we feel uncomfortable with silence or unsure of ourselves. Unfortunately, they'll distract your audience and make you sound uncertain. Replace them with a pause.

Practice pausing to create anticipation, suspense, drama and to evoke emotion and meaning – even when speaking in a small group or a meeting.

Pace
Speaking too quickly, or too slowly, can impact your ability to be heard.

Speaking too quickly is a common sign of nerves. When presenting, we should always aim to speak slower than usual. Sometimes this can seem very slow and even a bit strange, but your audience needs time to keep up (especially if they're unfamiliar with your subject).

Tip #19 Speak at an effective pace

On the other hand, you might find your natural speaking voice is quite slow. Be careful that this doesn't make you seem nervous or unsure; this can give the impression you lack energy, or worse still, that you're unprepared. Speaking at an effective pace helps you to maintain audience engagement. I've found it useful to record myself rehearsing. You could also seek feedback from a trusted friend.

Projection
There are a few factors that can impact the volume of your voice; some of us speak too softly, and others speak too loudly. It's a good idea to ask for feedback from a friend about your projection, as we are often unaware of how we sound.

Nerves, of course, are a major factor that may affect projection. Self-belief, too, is important. If you don't believe you deserve to be heard, that what you have to say is important and matters, you're likely to speak more softly. And of course, there are technical considerations, like the acoustics of the venue itself.

Bring your voice to life

When you give a presentation, you often need to speak louder than usual. A starting point is to be aware of the acoustics and size of the venue. This is particularly the case if the venue is unfamiliar to you. Be sure to do a sound check to make sure you can be heard. If you're using a microphone, ensure you know how to use it – preferably before you begin. For more specific information on how to use microphones effectively, see Chapter 7.

Tip #20 Test your voice projection in the venue

If you're not using a microphone, make sure you can be heard all the way to the back row. Check this before you begin. Be aware of competing noises such as air-conditioning, lawn mowing outside the room or a noisy meeting close by. If necessary, raise your voice further or pause until the noise subsides.

At the other end of the spectrum, some people are not aware they speak loudly and intensely. If you do this consistently, it can be quite wearing on your audience. Not only does speaking loudly distract your audience from hearing the words you're saying, but it can also strain your voice in a longer presentation. If you tend to speak loudly, you'll not need to project as much when speaking into a microphone.

Tip #21 Vary your pace and projection

I attended a workshop with Rory Vaden, thought leader and finalist of the World Champion of Public Speaking in 2014. He explained that to bring life and magic to your presentations, the trick is to use the four 'quadrants of vocal variety'.

Vaden's quadrants of vocal variety

SLOWER AND LOUDER Be authoritative; command respect	FASTER AND LOUDER Create excitement; be animated
SLOWER AND SOFTER Add authenticity and endearment	FASTER AND SOFTER Create anticipation and impact

Rather than speaking with the same volume and speed, Vaden's approach is to shift between quadrants. Doing this creates interest, suspense and emotion and helps you keep the attention of your audience. For example, if you slow your pace and increase your volume, you'll find you speak with authority. This gains the attention of your audience or shows an authoritative character in a story. Teachers and trainers often use this technique without having to say 'please pay attention' because the change attracts the attention of the inattentive. If you increase your pace and volume, this can create excitement.

Use the quadrants of vocal variety to experiment with pace and projection. This will work most effectively when complemented with the appropriate body language to bring your message to life.

Your accent need not be a barrier

Have you ever felt frustrated that your accent may be a barrier to communicating clearly? I've worked with people with a variety of accents. A common concern is they don't feel heard, which impacts their confidence and often results in them keeping quiet through fear of embarrassment or being misunderstood.

 Tip #22 Enunciate and rephrase to support understanding

To ensure you're understood by people who are unfamiliar with your accent:

- enunciate individual words and syllables
- break up words with multiple syllables as these tend to be the most difficult to understand
- be aware that your pitch may impact your clarity
- slow your pace considerably so that words don't run together but can be articulated individually
- pause and accentuate keywords
- rephrase sentences when you know your audience hasn't understood you. It may be a particular word or pattern of words they haven't grasped.

CLIENT STORY: My accent is no longer a barrier

Elodie sought coaching with me because she felt her accent was an obstacle to her credibility and having a strong voice in meetings. She often wondered if her colleagues 'politely' misunderstood her without saying anything. This was accentuated in online meetings, which she felt amplified her challenges with projection and diction. She wanted to be clear and succinct in her communication whilst honouring her accent.

After a few coaching sessions experimenting with breathing and gaining awareness of the four Ps, Elodie's confidence grew. She now doesn't hesitate to speak up in meetings and share her ideas with colleagues.

'Kerry provided me with excellent strategies to address these issues, including ways to structure my thinking, but also slowing down my pace, purposeful pausing, stressing keywords and adjusting pitch when I speak.' (Elodie, Strategic Research Development Manager, 2020)

Emphasis and tone

By emphasising specific words within a sentence, you increase meaning and emotion. This helps bring your story to life.

 Tip #23 Emphasise keywords to create meaning

The words you choose to emphasise within a sentence can vary its meaning. Have a look at this example. It shows how the meaning shifts depending upon the words you emphasise – even though the sentence hasn't changed at all.

Sentence	Differentiated meaning based on word emphasis
<u>I</u> was born in Australia.	Emphasis on 'I' can mean compared to all of you who were not.
I **<u>was</u>** born in Australia.	Emphasis on 'was' can mean – don't you believe me?
I was **born** in Australia.	Emphasis on 'born' can mean – I was born there but don't live there now.
I was born in **<u>Australia</u>**.	Emphasis on 'Australia' can be in response to a direct question about where you were born.

Altering the tone of your voice can also change the meaning of a sentence. Try saying the simple sentence 'I want to go' using different emotions and moods, such as joy, hurt, fear, sarcasm, sadness, disgust and even seductiveness. Notice how you automatically change which words you emphasise. Your body language and facial expressions are probably changing, too, as you alter the pace, projection, pitch and tone of your voice to convey emotion and meaning.

Breathing

It's common to use upper chest breathing when you feel nervous. This can have a negative impact on your vocal quality, which isn't preferable when you're trying to sound confident and professional. Upper chest breathing creates a breathiness in the voice; it's especially noticeable when you're using a microphone. Diaphragm breathing will alleviate these problems.

 Tip #24 Diaphragm breathing for pitch, pace, projection and clarity

Upper chest breathing reduces your ability to vary the pitch of your voice. More often than not, upper chest breathing creates a higher pitch, making you sound less confident. It can also cause you to speak too quickly as you try to catch your breath, and it restricts your voice projection. Mumbling is another trap to avoid. We mumble when we don't open our mouth wide enough or close it too quickly. Airflow is constricted, and the result is a lack of clarity.

Try calming your nerves before you present by relaxing your shoulders, chest, and throat. Shoulder rolls, head rotations and stretches can make an enormous difference. See Chapter 2 for more strategies about managing your nerves.

Posture

Good posture helps you project your voice whether you're standing or sitting; it ensures you breathe more freely from your diaphragm. When standing to present, plant your feet parallel and hip-width apart with weight evenly distributed, soft knees and relaxed shoulders. When sitting, sit up straight with your shoulders back and relaxed. Folding arms or crossing your legs can squash your diaphragm, giving your voice less power and authority.

Tip #25 Maintain good posture

If you have the choice, always choose to stand. Your voice will have more authority, and you'll have more opportunity to influence. If the situation allows, you could even pause and walk to a new spot to keep your body agile, further supporting your voice. Always move with purpose and avoid wandering.

When gesturing, be careful not to drop your hands before you finish a sentence, because this may also cause you to reduce the volume and clarity of your voice, making the end of your sentence less effective.

Warm up your voice

Bodycoat (2018) explained that professional singers, actors and presenters warm up their tongue, throat, jaw and cheeks before they perform, to ensure vocal quality and avoid straining their voices.

Her workshop included simple exercises that you can do at home or just before giving a speech, presenting an idea at a meeting, or participating in a job interview. Make sure you at least avoid being silent for the half-hour leading up to an event. Just talking will warm up your voice.

Tip #26 Warm up your voice before presenting

Reading anything aloud is helpful for your voice. This could include novels, plays, poems or tongue twisters.

Tongue twisters are particularly useful for developing enunciation and for warming up the jaw and tongue.

Try the following:

- Find tongue twisters that emphasise different vowels and consonants.
- Practice these aloud, exaggerating the vowels and consonants.
- Observe and become familiar with how each vowel and consonant is formed, i.e. what your lips, jaw and tongue do when you pronounce each of these.
- Say the vowels whilst keeping your tongue still. Note that the tongue helps you to deliver vowel sounds.
- Repeat the tongue twister without exaggerating the vowels and consonants.

If you're serious about developing your vocal capability, voice coaches can provide training programs specific to your needs. I suggest you listen to a recording of your voice before you embark upon a program; this will help you to identify strengths and areas for improvement, and you'll be able to measure your progress by doing follow up recordings.

> *"Practice varying the 4 Ps to bring your voice to life:*
> *Pitch,*
> *Pause,*
> *Pace,*
> *Projection"*

Summary of tips for bringing your voice to life

Tip #16　Vary the pitch of your voice.

Tip #17　Avoid using a rising inflection when not asking a question.

Tip #18　Use purposeful pausing.

Tip #19　Speak at an effective pace.

Tip #20　Test your voice projection in the venue.

Tip #21　Vary your pace and projection.

Tip #22　Enunciate and rephrase to support understanding.

Tip #23　Emphasise keywords to create meaning.

Tip #24　Diaphragm breathing for pitch, pace, projection and clarity.

Tip #25　Maintain good posture.

Tip #26　Warm up your voice before presenting.

Part III
You deserve to be heard

My job as a coach is diverse. People seek coaching for a range of reasons – but it inevitably comes down to not feeling heard. My clients often tell me they feel:

- scared to share ideas in meetings
- terrified about pitching themselves or going blank in interviews
- inadequate and experience 'imposter syndrome' when asked to present at a conference
- out of their depth when presenting or meeting online
- embarrassed about giving a speech at a wedding or at a colleague's farewell
- uncertain about the responsibilities and characteristics of an effective MC
- fearful about approaching strangers at networking events
- misunderstood when presenting technical information outside of their field
- unconfident about being a leader who can communicate with conviction and clarity.

The following chapters provide strategies for achieving confidence and clarity in these situations.

Wherever and whenever you communicate, you deserve to be heard.

5 IN A MEETING

There are many parallels between communicating at a meeting and presenting to an audience. Both require you to:

- capture the audience's attention
- appear confident
- communicate with clarity
- use body language effectively
- engage with your audience
- build relationships and instil trust
- speak with authority and credibility
- speak passionately and authentically
- influence your audience.

Have you ever felt frustrated at a meeting because you didn't get the chance to have your say? Have you been asked a question and not been given adequate time to think about your answer?

You're not alone. I frequently hear these problems from my clients. If you appear confident, you're less likely to be shut down, and more likely to be actively listened to and called upon for your opinion.

Preparing strategically

Despite the many unknown elements of meetings, you can do plenty of preparation to give you a sense of control and confidence. To maximise your opportunities to be heard, prepare your content as well as your approach. A major difference between communicating at a meeting compared with a typical presentation is that meetings are usually conducted sitting down.

In a meeting

Choose to stand if you're asked in advance to present at a meeting. Standing will give you more presence and allow you to adopt a strong stance. You'll look and feel more confident. You can move around the space freely and more actively engage with the audience.

Some clients worry that standing may appear inappropriate or even aggressive. I suggest they locate themselves in a spot where it doesn't look odd to stand. This could be near a whiteboard where you can illustrate your point or idea.

Sitting invariably lends itself to poorer posture than standing. It's easy to slouch in a chair and to use closed body language such as crossing arms and legs or touching your face, all of which can contribute to you looking less confident. Diaphragm breathing is harder to achieve when seated, especially if you're slouching. You may be more likely to breathe from your upper chest, which will have a negative effect on your voice projection and clarity.

Tip #27 Consider standing to present

Arrive early to the meeting to position yourself strategically. For example, if you're feeling nervous, place yourself close to a trusted friend or ally. When you begin to speak, look at them for a friendly smile of reassurance. If they smile at you, this is a catalyst to encourage you to smile, which will help you relax and be more engaging.

There may also be people in the meeting who you want to target. Try seating yourself next to or opposite them so you can easily speak to them.

Avoid sitting near those who may not support your views or who may be less respectful. If you can't see their reaction when you speak, you're less likely to be distracted by any negativity.

Tip #28 Position yourself strategically

If you're having trouble jumping into a conversation that's in progress, you can give non-verbal signals that you have something to contribute. It can also be useful to seat yourself where you're in easy view of the chairperson. Non-verbal signals can include shifting slightly forward in your chair, giving direct eye contact to the chairperson, and putting your hands on the table in front of you. When seated like this, it's easier for you to use confident and open gestures to help influence the group with your idea. For example, you can use open palm gestures and inclusive eye contact to show your intention to include, welcome and involve everyone in what you're sharing.

Watch for the non-verbal signals of others. Those who are likely to agree with you may nod their head, return your eye contact, or even tilt their head ever so subtly to the side. Make sure you give your focus and attention to the people who are actively listening. Try not to get too caught up with those who are less engaged. These people may cross their arms, be looking at their phones or whispering to someone else in the room while you're speaking. Don't allow one or two potentially less-engaged people to distract you. Don't personalise the non-verbals of a seemingly less-engaged person as they may have other priorities or stresses that are dominating their thinking, which may not be, and usually aren't, a reflection on you.

Tip #29 Observe the non-verbal cues of yourself and others

The key isn't to focus on a single non-verbal cue as you may misread a situation, and it may influence your ability to demonstrate your confidence. For example, the person who's feeling cold may have their arms crossed but simultaneously give you direct eye contact and nod in agreement.

Your reaction is more important than your answer

It's common to be asked unexpected questions that you don't know the answer to or can't answer easily within a short timeframe. Unexpected questions can be one of the most daunting and nerve-wracking challenges of meetings. If you look uncertain or nervous, you'll be treated differently, which may impact your ability to be heard. If you panic because you fear your integrity may be in jeopardy, it may cause a brain freeze and make it more difficult for you to think clearly about your answer.

Unfortunately, you may feel that you have to be an expert on everything and answer any question with confidence to show your worth. Remember to give yourself a break and know that it's okay not to always know the answer. It's also okay to say that you don't know the answer.

Take the time to observe others in meetings who come across as confident and authoritative. What do they do when they're asked challenging questions? They may:

- refer to someone else
- promise to find out for the next meeting
- volunteer to follow up with an email
- change the subject.

Using these strategies with confidence ensures you retain your authority in a meeting.

I've had clients tell me they've missed opportunities to answer questions or contribute to meeting discussions. Sometimes meetings can be fast paced; sometimes others seem to dominate the discussion. Clients have even told me examples of how their colleagues expressed the same idea as them, but with more confidence and authority. It can feel like someone else is getting credit for your ideas. The experience of missing opportunities to communicate can be incredibly disempowering and contribute to diminished confidence.

To find your voice in meetings, you may need to be innovative and think outside the square to be heard. For example, you may be more influential with your written communication than your oral communication, so take advantage of this strength. Communicate your ideas in writing before a meeting in anticipation that it may be discussed. Or you might choose to share your thoughts in writing after the meeting if you weren't able to express your idea verbally.

Tip #30 Find alternative ways to be heard

If there's an agenda for a meeting, gather your thoughts on specific agenda items, so you come prepared and don't have to think on the spot. If there's no agenda, prepare what you'd like to share so that you're ready. For example, if you're asked to give an update on your project or identify where you may require support, you can have these answers ready about your current work priorities. Other options include approaching a colleague after a meeting to request a further discussion or sending an email once you've had time to process your thoughts. Be sure to be solution-oriented and strategic in your approach, rather than showing or expressing that you felt defeated.

In a meeting

Don't put pressure on yourself to make a major contribution at every meeting. You may notice that people who dominate meetings don't always have useful and constructive things to say. Sometimes it's beneficial to be silent and to listen carefully so you can hear others' views.

When you're put on the spot and feeling nervous, you might mistakenly believe you have to answer a question the split second after it's been asked. It's often not the case, and it's helpful to buy yourself some time to think of how you could answer the question.

Tip #31 Give yourself time to think

You can use the following strategies to buy yourself time:

- Pause and breathe from your diaphragm to calm your nerves and clear your head.
- Repeat or paraphrase the question to ensure you've heard and understood it clearly.
- Make direct eye contact with the person who asked the question and then make eye contact with everyone else in the meeting. As you conclude your answer, return your gaze to the person who asked the question.
- Admit confidently and unapologetically if you don't know the answer. Assure your audience that you'll find out. Alternatively, you can refer the question to someone else in the room.
- Signal that you're ready to speak by sitting forward in your seat.
- Use open palm gestures as a signal that you're welcoming your audience to listen and to support your answer.
- Don't pretend to know an answer; rather, orchestrate solutions for finding the answer.

Structuring an effective impromptu response

Providing structure to your response to impromptu questions has many benefits. Structures provide a framework that helps you be succinct, logical and easy to follow. Presenting a coherent and clear beginning, middle and end to your answer will help you avoid waffling and make it easier for your audience to understand and hear your thoughts. If you struggle with knowing how to begin, frameworks provide you with a mental model that you can use with a broad range of scenarios and questions and will make you appear more confident. Whilst you're working through the first part of a framework, you have more time to formulate the next part of your response. Structures also give you a clear signpost of when and how to end your response.

Below are some examples of frameworks that you can use in meetings to respond to impromptu questions.

Example 1: For questions that require your opinion:
- state your opinion
- give your reason
- share an example or story to illustrate your reason
- restate your opinion and offer a solution.

Example 2: For questions that require a project update:
- provide your answer in a chronological way; origins of the project, what you're currently doing, and next steps.

Example 3: For explaining a solution to a problem or ideas for moving forward, in three clear parts.

Audiences often feel comfortable with ideas expressed in three parts – especially if the time available is short or they seek quick solutions to a problem. To satisfy your audience, you could try to:

- express your solution in three steps
- describe three strategies, or
- put forward three ideas for the audience to discuss or choose from.

Example 4: When asked for your opinion where there are two potential options:

- outline one side of the argument with examples of why this argument is valid
- outline the other side of the argument with examples of why this argument is valid
- summarise your opinion on which option is most valid and make a recommendation.

Using this framework shows you have heard, understood, and considered alternative viewpoints to your own.

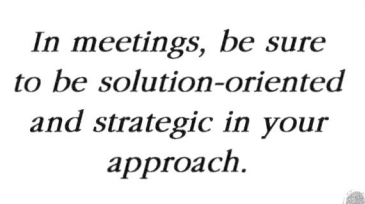

In meetings, be sure to be solution-oriented and strategic in your approach.

Summary of tips on how to be heard in meetings

Tip #27   Consider standing to present.

Tip #28   Position yourself strategically.

Tip #29   Observe the non-verbal cues of yourself and others.

Tip #30   Find alternative ways to be heard.

Tip #31   Give yourself time to think.

6 AT JOB INTERVIEWS

Many people fear job interviews. It can be confronting when you don't know what to expect. The idea of selling yourself and thinking on your feet can be daunting. Most people report that being under pressure in a contrived situation makes it hard to be yourself and demonstrate who you are and what you have to offer to your interviewers.

Preparing for your interview

Despite the many unknown elements of a job interview, there's plenty of preparation you can do to give you a sense of control and confidence.

Begin with researching the organisation and the role you're applying for by examining their website, searching for information and speaking with others. This will help you identify the organisation's strategic priorities, challenges, special projects and events. Information you glean from your research can be woven into your answers and show your genuine interest in the organisation, as well as showcase your initiative. By doing your homework, you may stand out from the rest.

You can also research types of questions that are typically asked for a role like yours. Many interview questions are predictable. Practice some interview answers before the big day.

 Tip #32 Research the organisation and role

Have questions and information prepared for the interviewers. This will show them that you've done your homework and will give you the chance to share important aspects about you that may have been missed via the interview questions.

Concrete examples and stories will engage your interviewers and make you more credible. They also make you more memorable than a candidate who just gives examples of what makes an effective team player for example, without demonstrating how they do it. Using personal stories will help you connect with your audience and make a lasting impression. Ultimately, how you make them feel will have more impact than what you make them think. The panel will certainly be assessing whether you can do the job, but they'll also be influenced by whether they like you or not.

Stories can make you more personable, help you illustrate why the job matters to you and how you'll be a positive contributor to the organisation. They can also give you the impetus to smile as you recount something important to you, which will help you be yourself.

Create a list of stories and examples that apply to different types of questions in different interviews. Have them ready for whatever question is thrown at you. In preparation for a particular interview, choose examples of how you've managed situations that align with anticipated questions. For example, if you think the panel may ask you how you contribute to teams, think about specific situations in current and previous jobs where you've demonstrated effective team skills.

 Tip #33 Prepare an inventory of stories

At job interviews

It can be helpful to hold a mock interview with a trusted friend, mentor or coach to practice responding to anticipated questions and manage gaps in your knowledge. It can also be useful to receive feedback about how you logically and succinctly structure your responses and how you come across in terms of your body language.

Tip #34 Participate in a mock interview

Practising your interview skills helps you avoid common mistakes. Don't assume your interviewer recalls the details of your resume or application. The interview may be held well after the short-listing process. Another common mistake is when you know people on the panel. Don't assume they know all that you do in your current role. You need to connect the dots for them and make connections with what you do and how your skills and experience will be valuable in the new position. Mock interviews can make the actual interview less daunting.

Managing your nerves

Many people report that being nervous in interviews is a barrier to them selling their credentials, experience, and value to the organisation. They often express that a lack of techniques to manage their nerves detracted from their ability to perform well.

If this is you, try using these easy-to-apply tips at your next interview.

Tip #35 Plan for a positive experience

Undertake some diaphragm breathing upon waking and throughout the day leading up to the interview to manage your nerves. Also, set yourself up for success by visualising how you want the interview to turn out or write down how you'd like it to play out.

When you arrive at the interview, take some deep breaths before entering the building and while you're waiting for your turn. (See Chapter 2 on diaphragm breathing and how to set yourself up for success).

Tip #36 Use open and confident body language

Whilst waiting, stand rather than sit. Avoid using your phone as this will encourage closed posture. If you're waiting in a private space, use this time to do some power posing to make you feel more confident and to set yourself up for a confident stance when your interviewers arrive. When someone enters the room to collect you, drop your hands from your waist to your sides, but maintain your strong and confident stance. Walk confidently to the interview room, and upon meeting each interviewer, look them directly in the eye and smile.

When you're invited to take a seat, ensure you sit up straight and be mindful of not slouching as the interview progresses. Keep your body language open to appear confident. This includes keeping your legs and arms uncrossed and avoiding touching your face and neck. If gesturing, use open palms to welcome your audience to engage with you and use descriptive gestures when giving examples or sharing stories.

At job interviews

Responding to questions with clarity and confidence

Many people mistakenly think they need to respond to a question the split second after being asked. This is not true. It's better for you and your audience if you take your time. Taking the time to think about your answer will communicate to your audience that you're not rattling off the first thing that comes into your head but that you're giving the consideration that the question deserves.

 Tip #37 Pause before responding

Pause and take a couple of diaphragm breaths while you think about your answer. To buy more time, consider repeating or rephrasing the question.

When you're ready to answer, sit slightly forward in your seat to give the signal to your audience that you're ready to speak. Begin your answer by giving eye contact to the person who asked the question, then after a few seconds, look at the others. As you summarise your answer, return your eye contact to the person who asked the question. This provides your interviewers with a clear cue that you've finished your answer. (See Chapter 3 on effective use of eye contact).

If you don't understand a question when you first hear it, don't panic. If you're finding a question difficult, it's likely other applicants may also be stumped, so don't beat yourself up or let this impact your confidence. Pause and breathe so you can think clearly.

If you still can't figure out what's being said, don't make the mistake of pretending. Ask the interviewer to rephrase the question. If you can partially answer a question, go ahead and do so. If you have no idea, ask if you can come back to it so you can move on to another question where you can have the opportunity to impress.

Often when nervous, it's difficult to know when to end your answer, resulting in waffling, going off the topic and even forgetting the question.

It can be useful to practice using structures to respond to questions. These allow you to have a clear opening and ending and include relevant stories in between. Be as succinct and structured as you can when answering the question.

 Tip #38 Practice structuring responses

At job interviews

Here are two ways to structure your response to the following interview question:

This role will require you to be an effective team player. Please explain how you will contribute to the team as an effective team player.

Structure 1: Chronological response

Previous job example: In my previous role, I demonstrated my ability to work effectively in a team by mentoring new staff members on how to undertake tasks.

Current job example: In my current role, team skills are particularly important because we have a very busy office and only a small team. Just recently, I could see my colleague was under pressure with deadlines, and I needed to drop what I was doing to help. If I hadn't helped him, the deadlines may not have been met.

For the position I am applying for: If successful in winning this position, I'll contribute to my team by understanding each person's role and peak milestones within the team so I can be flexible and step in to help others who need support. I understand the strength of the team depends on everyone contributing to the team goals.

Structure 2: Giving your opinion and backing it up with examples

Stating your opinion: I believe an effective team player appreciates all members of the team and is committed to a collective goal. If one team member isn't sensitive to the needs of the rest of the team, this can create a weak link.

Giving an example: For example, in a previous job, we worked on a project where each new step relied on the successful completion and communication of the previous step. One of my colleagues was so caught up in their part of the project they forgot to communicate with the rest of us. This held up the progress of the project and put others under pressure to complete their part. I approached the person in question and discovered they were not aware or didn't understand how their actions impacted others. I helped them communicate and connect all the pieces and suggested to my manager that we hold more frequent meetings to update the project's status, and this improved communications.

If you'd like access to a cheat sheet about how to be successful in an interview, visit the following link on my website:

www.completecommunicationcoach.com.au/YDTBH

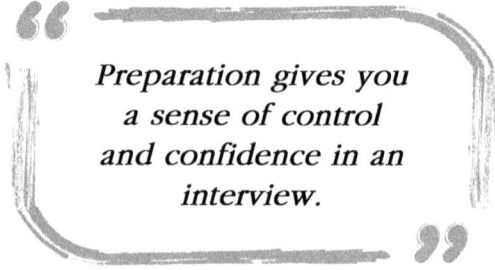

> *Preparation gives you a sense of control and confidence in an interview.*

At job interviews

Summary of tips for job interviews

Tip #32   Research the organisation and role.

Tip #33   Prepare an inventory of stories.

Tip #34   Participate in a mock interview.

Tip #35   Plan for a positive experience.

Tip #36   Use open and confident body language.

Tip #37   Pause before responding.

Tip #38   Practice structuring responses.

7 AS A PRESENTER

Have you ever avoided giving a presentation at a conference or at work because you thought you weren't good enough?

Preparing for and giving inspired and memorable presentations sounds daunting – but it can be done. Don't let fear or a sense of inadequacy hold you back from presenting to others. Don't avoid opportunities to showcase your ideas or your research. This chapter will provide you with the tools to prepare and present an inspiring and professional presentation.

What's in it for your audience?

A presentation without a specific purpose is like a journey without a destination. It's important to remember your presentation isn't about you, but about what your audience can gain from listening to you. Often the main purpose of a conference presentation is to inform or educate an audience as well as to persuade them to act. Your presentation needs to:

- gain the attention and curiosity of the audience
- present a problem and feasible solution(s)
- help the audience imagine the solution(s)
- persuade the audience to take action.

 Tip #39 Ensure your message is clear and relevant to your audience

As a presenter

If your audience isn't engaged, they'll struggle to understand your message and won't be inspired to take action. Be specific and focussed with your purpose and have a clear message for your audience. Your message needs to make sense, add value and matter to them. In other words, think from the audience's perspective.

To do this, you'll need to know who your audience is and why they may be attending the conference. Your presentation should complement the conference theme and be tailored to the audience. If you're writing a submission to present, do your research before you write to increase your chances of being chosen. These are the sorts of things you should consider:

- What's the conference for?
- What are current and potential issues for the industry/organisation?
- How many people will attend?
- What is the likely demographic breakdown of the audience, e.g. gender, age, social, political and ethnic backgrounds?
- Are you aware of your audience's expectations?
- How has the conference been promoted?

When preparing your presentation, state your point or message to yourself in one or two sentences. If you can't say this clearly to yourself, you won't make it clear for your audience. Write your purpose and message on the back of a business card and stick it on your computer while you're in the process of preparing. This will help keep you focussed and prevent you from moving off into other tangents that might interest you but may not be relevant for the audience. If it's not relevant to your audience, you will not be heard.

Designing content and structure

Writing for a presentation requires a different approach to writing something that's intended to be read. Often presenters are keen to share *all* of their wisdom or research in one sitting, which, to them, mistakenly is their purpose. Attempting to share it all can be overwhelming and even boring.

Tip #40 Be prepared to cull content

Rehearse your presentation so you can time its length. Be prepared to cull content that doesn't support your message, or which is unnecessarily repetitive. If you go over time, this can throw out the entire conference or meeting agenda or eat into the next speaker's allocated time. On the other hand, if you finish early, you can include extra question time or have other topics up your sleeve to lengthen your presentation in the moment.

Your introduction should be punchy, interesting, and delivered with energy. This will ensure you grab the audience's attention and connect with them in the first few seconds.

Tip #41 Grab the audience's attention with your introduction

The introduction could include asking a question, presenting a story, using an inspirational quote, singing a song or using a prop. All of these options will impact your audience better than starting with 'Today my presentation is about …'. Memorise your introduction to allow you to focus on smiling and engaging with your audience.

As a presenter

Your presentation should be structured in a way that's easy to navigate. Think of it as a map and ensure it follows a logical structure. This could include using clear transitions that glue the presentation together and providing segues from one main point to another. The use of pausing and keywords, phrases and sentences can cue the audience to be ready to move on with you.

Tip #42 Structure your presentation logically

The rule of three main components is usually an effective guide for the suitable amount to share in one presentation.

If you cover too much content, you may overwhelm or confuse your audience, or your message may be clouded by the volume of content.

When planning your content, find out who else is presenting and their topics, the order of the presentations and where you appear on the agenda. Read the bios of other presenters to avoid duplication. Conference audiences often enjoy a logical flow of presentations so that the agenda harmoniously hangs together, supporting the conference's theme and intended purpose. If you're the first presenter after lunch, the audience may need an energiser to help them refocus to ensure you'll be heard.

Tip #43 Conclude with a thought-provoking message or call to action

Your conclusion creates a lasting impression – make sure it's strong and memorable. You could offer a thought-provoking quote, statistic, or anecdote, or present a call to action with clear strategies for your audience to follow.

To close the loop, you can work out a way to tie your closing cleverly and creatively to the opening. This provides a neat finish and a clear reminder and reinforcement of your message.

Communicating with event organisers and the MC

Ensure you have clear expectations of what you want to achieve from speaking at a conference, meeting, or other events. Communicate this clearly with organisers and the Master of Ceremonies (MC) before and during the event. This will give you some control over how they promote you in event marketing. If you don't, it may impact your credibility during and after the event.

Tip #44 Provide a bio for promotions and an introduction to the MC

If you have the opportunity, provide the text you want included in the promotional materials to the event organisers. Also, provide an introduction about yourself and a brief summary of the content of your presentation to the MC. Your introduction should reflect how qualified you are to present on the topic by outlining your credentials and background, so the audience knows who you are.

The MC's role is to spark interest in the audience but not to give away your content. The MC is a very busy role, so if you don't communicate your expectations clearly, you may find the MC presents what's quick and easily accessible to them, which may be what's on the agenda or in the conference booklet.

Research the venue

Presenting can be nerve-wracking. The venue is often unfamiliar and may even be interstate or overseas.

Familiarise yourself with the venue as much as possible. Find out which room your presentation will be held in and arrange a visit in person if possible. At the very least, look at the venue website.

Aim to get a clear vision of what to expect and the environment in which you'll be presenting. Find out how the room will be laid out, which is commonly theatre style, where the audience sits in rows facing the stage, or cabaret style, where the audience sits around tables.

Tip #45 Familiarise yourself with the venue

If you're in a smaller room, without a microphone, you may need to project your voice to the back. If your voice is typically quiet, remember to practice diaphragm breathing to support your voice.

If you're presenting on a stage, you may find you'll be presenting to a large audience in a large space. Make sure you can be heard and that you're comfortable and confident using a microphone.

Using microphones

Depending on the size and acoustics of the venue, you may need a microphone, which is usually organised by the event planners. Make sure you familiarise yourself with it well before you present.

There are multiple types of microphones. Find out what style to expect as these may impact your presentation in different ways. Some event organisers or venues can provide you with a particular microphone type on request. If this is the case, request a lapel or headset microphone as these offer the most flexibility.

If possible, practice using a microphone in advance, and always arrange a sound check before you present, even though technical people are usually on hand should something go wrong during the presentation.

Your choice of microphone may impact what you can wear on the day of your presentation. For example, it's best to attach a lapel microphone to a tie, a jacket, a top with a medium to low neckline or a shirt. Avoid tee-shirts, high-neck tops, scarves and dresses without a belt. For a headset microphone, it is useful to wear a jacket to hide the transmitter, which is usually attached to the back of your pants or skirt.

Issues to be aware of when choosing a microphone

Types of microphones	Benefits	Issues to consider
MOBILE MICROPHONES	Allow you to move around the stage so that you can easily engage with different parts of the audience.	If you go to the bathroom, ensure the microphone is turned off.
Lapel microphone: A small device that you attach to your clothing.	Allows you to gesture with both hands.	Be careful not to bump the microphone when gesturing as this may cause sound interference.

As a presenter

Types of microphones	Benefits	Issues to consider
Headset microphone: A headset microphone, made famous by pop singer Madonna, is a small device that you attach to your ears. The voice piece sits forward to the side of your mouth.	Allows you to gesture with both hands. The microphone remains in the same position when you move your head, resulting in consistent sound quality.	Be careful not to bump the microphone when gesturing as this may cause sound interference.
Hand-held microphone	As it's carried in your hand, there are no limitations about the clothing that you wear.	Limits your ability to gesture with both hands. Hold it about 5 centimetres from your mouth like an ice-cream. Take note of the sound quality of other speakers as they may be holding the microphone too close or too far away.
STATIC/FIXED MICROPHONE *Gooseneck microphone*	If you wish to use the lectern, then the microphone is conveniently there for you in one spot.	Participate in a sound-check to ensure you can be heard from all parts of the room. You will be required to stand behind the lectern for your entire presentation. This may limit your ability to engage directly with your audience.

Preparing and rehearsing

Typically, conference presentations are conducted behind a lectern with the gooseneck microphone attached. Many presenters prefer this traditional presentation method as they can easily change slides at the lectern and have their notes in front of them.

You're not compelled to use a lectern just because it's what others do. Some of the best presentations are by those who step in front of the lectern and connect directly with their audience. If you have the courage to step away from the lectern, this can give you authority and help you stand out from the rest. Moving around the stage is much easier with a mobile microphone, and you'll connect in a much more personal way with your audience.

 Tip #46 You're not compelled to use a lectern

Inviting participation is a valuable technique to engage your audience, and it's much more effective if you're not behind a lectern. You can move around the stage using stagecraft and map your presentation. This means you can anchor your three main points on different parts of the stage, working from your right to your left (mirror image for your audience). It is recommended that you finish your presentation by reinforcing your message downstage centre. This is known as the power spot on the stage where you deliver the most important parts of your presentation.

With no lectern, you're free to use a range of gestures that will help you to emphasise points, tell stories and appeal to your audience. Note that in a very large venue, your gestures need to be larger than you'd typically use in a presentation to make sure the back row can see you.

As a presenter

Often conferences have breakout workshops held in smaller rooms with portable and adjustable lecterns. If you're presenting in one of these rooms, you may wish to have a lectern to put your notes on. It's advisable not to stand directly behind it as it creates an unnecessary physical barrier between you and your audience. You also run the risk of leaning on or gripping the lectern. This can make you look nervous and cause your upper body to look tense. Instead, angle the lectern to the side so you can glance at it as necessary, move around the room freely and connect with your audience. Often, portable lecterns allow you to adjust the height and angle, so take the time to get it in the position that suits you before you begin.

Regardless of which room you're presenting in, you need to be mindful of sightlines when moving around the speaking space. Make sure all audience members can see you at all times. You may need to test this out before the conference starts, so ask someone to stand in various parts of the room to ensure they can see you.

Be well rehearsed and prepared so you don't need to rely on your notes during your presentation. This will free you up to focus on your delivery. Not only should you rehearse what you want to say, but you should also rehearse when to change slides so your presentation flows. This will help you manage your nerves and focus on the presentation itself rather than worrying about what comes next.

Tip #47 Don't let notes compromise your delivery

Many of the people I coach tell me they've never done a presentation without notes. They're so fearful of forgetting what comes next that they desperately cling to their notes, just in case.

Often these are the very people who, when on the stage, realise they don't need their notes and hardly look at them at all.

Having word-for-word notes can create more havoc than help. If you lose your place, you have to find the exact word, which can increase your anxiety and be obvious to your audience. You also run the risk of losing the opportunity for building rapport and connection with the audience through direct eye contact. If you're constantly referring to your notes, it can be easy to forget to look up. When you do, it can seem cursory and unconvincing.

If you've structured your presentation into a logical sequence, you can memorise the sequence. Doing this allows you to recall which part, rather than which word, comes next. You can create major headings with dot points and keywords or phrases to prompt you under each heading. The following are some specific strategies. When using notes:

- avoid using capitals as they're harder to read
- use at least font size 14 so you don't have to strain to read
- leave plenty of white space for easy reading
- number pages and slides and indicate in your notes when to move to the next slide
- avoid clipping or stapling pages. It creates less noise if you can slide individual papers across the lectern.

Using visual aids

Using visual aids can complement your presentation if used well. On the flip side, they can detract from the quality of your presentation if they are not used well. Examples of visual aids may include props, whiteboards, flipcharts, models, and, most often, PowerPoint or Prezi.

As a presenter

Which comes first, your presentation or your slides?

The biggest mistake presenters make when using PowerPoint is to prepare their slides first and then script the presentation around them. The most powerful presenters take the opposite approach. They write their presentation first to develop a sound structure and content that supports their message and purpose. They then design visuals to support their message and purpose. It's important to have more to say than what appears on your slides as the audience are there to listen to you, not to read dense text.

Tip #48 Create your presentation before your slides

Effective PowerPoint presentations are those that include images and minimal text. Audiences remember visuals better than bullet points because images are more powerful and have a direct impact. If you choose your images carefully, they can support your message, help to tell your story and build an emotional connection with your audience.

Tip #49 Images are more powerful than text

Text-heavy slides can be boring and look cluttered. Your audience will tire of reading them, and they'll quickly forget the words. Your audience should be able to quickly glance at your slide, then immediately return their attention to you. They're attending the conference to hear from you. If they wanted to read dense slides, you could've sent them a copy and saved them time attending. Audiences are happy to see white space on slides and appreciate having some slides that include images only. This helps them to focus on you and what you have to say.

First and foremost, the font you use must be large enough for audiences to read clearly without effort – regardless of where they're sitting. Many experts suggest that fonts for large headings should be no smaller than font size 24. Some types and colours are more challenging to read, especially if not sufficiently contrasted with the background. Use font types that are easy to read and avoid using a range of different fonts. Don't use different colours, bold or underline text for the sake of it, but rather only to emphasise key points and messages. Use charts and tables that are easy to see. Avoid placing too many charts or tables on one slide.

You'll lose engagement with your audience if they're straining to see. Use alternatives such as providing handouts, emailing slides or just show a portion of your data. Summarise the data on charts and tables to highlight what you want the audience to focus on. Avoid excessive use of animation to bring words in and out of slides; this can be distracting and annoying.

Don't talk immediately when the text appears on the screen. Allow a few seconds for the audience to read before talking as they may not be actively listening. Be sure to rehearse with the slides so you're familiar with the sequence.

Don't read your presentation slides word for word. The audience will read the slides while you're talking rather than focus on you. You should also make sure you avoid turning your back on your audience to look at the projected screen. If the slides are visible on a laptop in front of you, there should be no reason to turn your back.

 Tip #50 Don't read your slides word for word

As a presenter

Remote clickers can be a handy presentation tool. Some remotes can be placed in your pocket so you can just hit your pocket to change your slide. Others allow you to blank out your screen for a period, giving you time to talk directly to your audience. This redirects attention to you – especially if you want to emphasise a critical point.

Another helpful feature is the timer that some remotes include. Alternatively, there are mobile phone apps that allow you to keep track of time (don't forget to turn your ring tone off). Be sure to put your remote clicker down when you're not using it; this will free you up to gesture with both hands without waving the clicker in the air.

If you choose to move away from your lectern, be sure not to stand in front of your slides. You'll block your audience's view and potentially cast a distracting light over your face.

Avoid standing in front of the screen

Relying on technology for your presentation without a backup plan can be risky. Arrive early enough to test and be familiar with the equipment. Ensure your device is fully charged and you have backup batteries for your remote.

 Tip #51 Have a technology backup plan

You don't have control over the internet or whether a globe cuts out on a projector halfway through your presentation, so you need to have a Plan B. This should include bringing a hard copy of your presentation slides with you. Most importantly, pause, breathe and compose yourself. The audience doesn't need to know that disaster has struck. You should be so familiar with your material that the show can go on without the technology.

> *Your presentation needs to make sense, add value and matter to the audience.*

As a presenter

Summary of tips for presentations

Tip #39 Ensure your message is clear and relevant to your audience.

Tip #40 Be prepared to cull content.

Tip #41 Grab the audience's attention with your introduction.

Tip #42 Structure your presentation logically.

Tip #43 Conclude with a thought-provoking message or call to action.

Tip #44 Provide a bio for promotions and an introduction for the MC.

Tip #45 Familiarise yourself with the venue.

Tip #46 You're not compelled to use a lectern.

Tip #47 Don't let notes compromise your delivery.

Tip #48 Create your presentation before your slides.

Tip #49 Images are more powerful than text.

Tip #50 Don't read your slides word for word.

Tip #51 Have a technology backup plan

8 ON ONLINE PLATFORMS

Whether we like it or not, communicating online has become a new and unexpected norm. Since the outbreak of COVID-19, many businesses have discovered the benefits of working online, and many of us have enjoyed the convenience (and the challenges) of working from home. Communicating online can make it easier to communicate across state and national borders and has opened up new opportunities for many who may have been disadvantaged by distance.

I'm guessing many of you were thrown in the deep end. That there was probably an expectation you'd suddenly participate in meetings and conduct presentations online with limited, if any, training on how to engage audiences on this very different platform.

For those who are competent using online platforms, I urge you to understand that not all of your potential clients or colleagues may feel comfortable and skilled in this area. You may need to support others to take this journey with you. This may mean refining your skills so others, who may be less confident than you, will trust, be influenced by, and engage with you.

You may be comforted to know many of the effective face-to-face communication strategies also apply when on camera. This chapter reinforces such strategies and gives some tips specific to the video medium. If you follow them, you'll provide the best possible experience for you and your audience when communicating online.

This chapter will help you to:

- participate in online meetings, interviews and presentations with a live audience
- create pre-recorded information videos or online courses
- engage with audiences when teaching and training online.

Conquering your fear of the camera

Compared with communicating face-to-face, it can feel nerve-wracking to speak via a camera. Many of us feel uncomfortable with how we look and sound on camera. Those who produce videos may be concerned about the impact a video may have on their reputation. Fear of technology due to inexperience and a lack of know-how can also be a barrier to confident online communication.

The strategies that calm your nerves and help you appear relaxed when communicating face-to-face, work equally well on camera. These include diaphragm breathing and effective use of body language; your audience won't know you're feeling uncomfortable. These will also help you communicate with credibility and authority in your field of expertise. See Chapter 2 for a detailed explanation of how to use these strategies.

If you're a self-confessed technophobe, you may be using this as an excuse to avoid online communication. Some people lack experience because they were not born in the age of computer technology, or simply do not have access to the same resources as others. I empathise with your fear and feelings of disempowerment. This is a real barrier for many of us. My advice to you is, yet again, be prepared to put yourself out of your comfort zone, to take a risk and to learn something new. I'm not suggesting you do this alone though. Many of us have family or friends who are technical whizzes, and we need to reach out to them to seek help. Alternatively, consider using a mentor or coach who can effectively teach you how to use popular online programs. Each time you're exposed to such technologies, it will become a little easier. You may even find a particular program is a lot easier to use than you thought, and it creates myriad opportunities you may have spent a lifetime avoiding.

Tip #52 Don't use being a technophobe as an excuse

To eliminate some of the fear, ensure you attend to the areas of technology that you have control over by preparing your equipment – charge batteries, undertake sound and other technical checks. But always have a Plan B in case the technology fails you in the moment. A great strategy is to have someone on hand with technical skills who can troubleshoot and fix any problems. Don't panic; it happens to the best of us. If you deal with it calmly and professionally (as you would if something goes wrong in a live presentation or meeting), your credibility will remain intact.

Working with the camera

This section explains:
- ♦ how to use the camera so you can be a powerful and influential presenter
- ♦ ways to work within the camera frame
- ♦ benefits and limitations when working on camera.

On online platforms

There are some distinct differences between building trust and connecting with your audience on camera compared to presenting to a live audience. The main difference is that, online, the camera limits the space you can use. When presenting to a face-to-face audience, especially a large one, you can use the entire stage area. You have the freedom to use a broad range of body language to convey your message. However, when on camera, if you choose to use the same size space and have your whole body in the camera frame, you're likely to be too far away from the camera for the audience to see your eyes and facial expressions.

When standing, the optimal frame should be no lower than just below the waist. This allows you to move within your frame but also use a full range of gestures.

Tip #53 Be aware of the camera frame

When sitting, it's important not to cut off the frame at an awkward position. You need to decide whether you cut off at the armpits or the waist, but not in between. If your frame is from the armpits up, you won't be able to freely use hand gestures as they may sweep in and out of the frame and be distracting. If your frame is from the waist up, use gestures more slowly and deliberately than you would for a live audience.

On camera, your eye contact and facial expressions are crucial. Make sure you know where the camera is located and make virtual eye contact by looking directly at it.

Tip #54 Look at the camera lens (not the screen)

When you are online with a live audience, it's natural to want to look at the faces on the screen. If you do this when speaking, you lose the opportunity to engage and connect. Visualise the ideal person in your audience and pretend the camera lens is that person. This will make it appear that you're looking directly at them. It will also help you to present with more energy.

If you're using a laptop, you may need to adjust its height and position so you're able to look directly at your camera. Prop up your laptop so your camera is at eye level and directly in front of you. Try placing it on a stand or pile of books so you're not looking down at the camera. If necessary, you may need to face it in another direction, so it doesn't show a profile view.

If you're referring to notes or a PowerPoint presentation, the camera should be positioned just above your screen or notes. This will look more natural and allow you to engage with the camera easily whilst glancing at your notes as needed. If notes are located to the side, it's distracting and awkward to watch someone's eyes flick to them. This can cause you to lose connection with your audience and appears unnatural.

Whatever device you use, understand its limitations and think about what'll work best for you and your audience.

Ask a friend to meet you online so you can place your camera in the optimal position. If you're working with multiple screens, place your webcam on top of the screen you'd like to face. You may find it helpful to put a small hole into a sticky note or a photo and stick this over the camera so the lens is poking through the hole. Use this as a prompt to remind you to focus on this spot. Undertake trial runs and get feedback so you can adopt the optimal position for your gaze.

On online platforms

The above image demonstrates the impact of engaging directly with the camera, considering your frame, being aware of distractions and the importance of using animated and friendly facial expressions. I invite you to consider who is the most and least engaging in this image and ask yourself why.

For example, the person bottom right is not engaged in the meeting and is blatantly checking his watch. The person top right of the screen may not be aware that someone is walking past, and her head is cut off at the top of frame; which is distracting to the audience. The person sitting at the bottom and centre would benefit from moving her camera to the screen she is sitting at so she can look directly at the camera. The person sitting middle left looks very serious; a smile would help him engage. The person in the centre is engaging with the camera extremely well. As more of her torso is showing, she can use hand gestures when she speaks, her smile is friendly, and she is sitting centrally with no distractions.

Performing without a live audience

One benefit of performing without a live audience is you have the opportunity to see and hear yourself on the screen, which allows you to adapt your presentation. Make sure you notice whether your voice is becoming flat, your facial expressions are not animated, or you're not looking directly into the camera. If you use dynamic, energetic facial expressions, this will help you connect with and emotively move your audience. Looking serious and speaking with a 'deadpan' face may also limit the variation in your voice and may result in your audience becoming bored and even ceasing to watch and listen to you. Facial expressions can be harder to read on camera, so be prepared to use them in an animated way to have the desired effect on your audience.

Another benefit of performing without a live audience is the opportunity to use close-up shots of your face. Being up close and personal can help you influence your audience as they'll feel you're speaking personally to them.

We often find the immediate feedback from a live audience energising; it can also be a useful means of gauging our impact. Of course, this depends on whether their video and audio are turned on. When there's no live audience, we have to create our own energy. If you anticipate that your audience may laugh when you use humour, remember to pause after your punchlines to allow time for the laughter to subside before you move on. The absence of pauses may result in your audience missing the next part of your presentation.

Going live: online teaching and training

Teaching and training online require a different approach to face-to-face interaction.

The key to maintaining engagement online is to encourage and facilitate as much interaction as possible. Your aim should be to promote active participation rather than passive listening and learning. Your workshop or training should include activities and encourage collaboration. These can be facilitated using functions within your online platform, such as chat facilities, live polls and whiteboards for documenting discussions. Encourage interaction through smaller group discussions that can be shared as a whole group. Programs like Zoom and Microsoft Teams have the capacity to create breakout rooms so smaller and separate discussions and activities can occur.

Tip #55 Encourage active participation

Breaking up your lessons into smaller chunks will also help you to maintain audience engagement. Attention spans online are much shorter, so aim to change it up as much as you can. For example, you could pose questions, ask students to respond on the written chat function, followed by sharing some answers verbally. You can include small group activities, share responses on the interactive whiteboard and ask students to annotate the documents you share. Short, interactive activities are the key to maintaining engagement. You'll also need to schedule more frequent breaks than you would when teaching face to face.

It's much harder to maintain engagement when using audio in the background of a PowerPoint slide document without being able to see your face. Try splitting your screen via spotlighting so your face is visible; this is more personal. Once you've finished sharing a document, bring your full face back to the screen so the audience focuses on you and you can see them. This gives you a much better opportunity to influence and connect with your audience.

If you'd like access to a cheat sheet entitled 'Seven Essential tips for engaging audiences in online presentations and meetings', visit: www.completecommunicationcoach.com.au/YDTBH

Preparing videos

This section focuses on overcoming your concerns about creating videos and the importance of being authentic and personable on camera.

Many people feel uncomfortable creating videos of themselves; they feel embarrassed about how they think they look or sound on camera. They fear seeming amateurish or just not good enough. Or they may procrastinate because they don't have specialised equipment, a dedicated budget or the ideal environment to make a video. These are the people who are most likely to procrastinate about making a video or who spend hours editing it. Does this sound like you?

Tip #56 Stop procrastinating; make a video

On online platforms

Many audiences don't expect a polished and carefully edited Hollywood production. They want to hear what you have to say. It's more important to your audience that you demonstrate authenticity and sincerity and that you develop trust. You can come across as professional without striving for a perfect video. Focus on connecting with your audience, using vibrant voice and facial expressions, and looking into the eyes of your audience through the camera lens. To be successful, you may need to curb your embarrassment, put your ego aside and let your personality shine through the camera. Smile, at least at the beginning and the end of your video, to help put you and your audience at ease and make you look approachable and friendly.

If you feel particularly uncomfortable staring at your camera, it can help to pair up with a colleague to have a conversation or an interview rather than staring directly at the camera. The process may be less confronting and more fun. Once you're feeling more comfortable working on camera, you can gradually progress to connecting directly with the camera lens, which is the most effective means of connecting with your audience.

How you set the scene for your video will impact the quality of your engagement and the frame you use. Will you be sitting at a desk, on a couch or in a standing position? If you choose to sit on a couch, you can create a more relaxed mood, potentially including other people in the shot for a conversation. Using a wider frame puts more of your torso on display. This will allow you to freely use hand gestures to describe concepts, appeal to your audience or tell stories. If you're in a seated position, be mindful not to slouch, as this gives the impression you lack confidence or professionalism. It's also important to think about the furniture you use.

For example, choose a seat that makes it easy to sit up straight and to look and feel comfortable. Think about your background too; make sure it doesn't distract the audience or detract from your professional demeanour.

 Tip #57 Set the scene for maximum impact

Another strategy to use to change the mood of your video is to create it in an outdoor setting. You'll feel more relaxed if seated in a nice garden rather than a clinical looking office. It allows you to breathe in some fresh air; this can help you feel calmer if you are feeling particularly nervous. It may also be more appealing and relaxing for some audiences to see videos filmed outside. Be aware of outdoor noises that may distract from what you're saying, and ensure you have adequate sound equipment.

We live in a fast-moving world where people are typically exposed to short pre-recorded and live videos on YouTube and social media platforms. Consider creating short videos of around three to ten minutes (depending on your audience's age) rather than longer ones to cater to shorter attention spans.

 Tip #58 Be concise with video content

Speak more slowly than you usually would and pause at the end of each section or point of your presentation. This will allow your audience to digest information more easily or take notes if they choose. Be concise with your content – when you slow it down and add pauses, it will be much longer than you might expect.

On online platforms

Hosting and participating in online meetings

This section covers how to host an online meeting and how to be an effective meeting participant.

The role of the online meeting host is to make sure everyone can be heard, and that information is effectively conveyed. If you want to encourage your audience to listen to your ideas or persuade them to action, look directly into the camera to build rapport and authority.

It's important for you as the host to set up meeting protocols and expectations. This will help participants use appropriate online meeting etiquette and use functions to ensure the meeting is a positive communication experience. For example, the host should monitor audio functions. It's customary when entering a meeting to mute your microphone; multiple microphones can cause interference and distorted and distracting sounds. However, it's polite and personable if the host can greet each participant as they enter the meeting, and for participants to have the opportunity to reply before muting their microphones.

 **Tip #59** Set up online meeting protocols

Once the meeting begins, the host can ask participants to mute themselves, or the host may choose to take control of the audio for everyone. This will deter multiple participants from talking at the same time. If a participant arrives late to the meeting, it's useful to encourage them to find a pause in the conversation or the chat function to let everyone know they've arrived – just as you would if they'd entered the room for a face-to-face meeting.

To make sure muting doesn't deter participants from contributing, the host can encourage them to unmute when they wish to speak. Alternatively, other functions that allow engagement, such as the chat and virtual hands-up function can be used.

In a very large meeting, it can be useful for the host to have a backup person to monitor the chat function as it can be a busy task on top of hosting the meeting. To help identify and respond to questions in the chat function efficiently, ask participants to prefix their questions with a 'Q' for a question and 'C' for comments. A further safety net the host can use to make sure someone doesn't go unnoticed, is to encourage participants to raise their hand the old-fashioned way. If they're not feeling included and get the impression that their input is not valued, this may deter them from participating in subsequent meetings.

It's up to the host to monitor the use of cameras in a meeting. The host should explain, if necessary, the benefits of connecting through their cameras. Participants should be respectfully encouraged to turn on their camera if possible (within bandwidth restrictions, camera availability and privacy needs).

If you notice the internet connection and clarity of video or audio is compromised for an individual, the host can ask that they turn their cameras off for a short period.

In addition to addressing technical glitches, it can be useful for some cameras to be turned off so that the focus can be on particular people. This should be monitored depending on the purpose of the meeting and the number of people participating. The host may also suggest the viewer settings that are most applicable for specific purposes. For example, if individuals are presenting in a meeting, it may be appropriate to focus more prominently on

On online platforms

individual presenters through speaker view. When all participants are encouraged to take part in the discussion, gallery view may be better as it ensures that all faces can be seen.

I recently ran an online workshop on how to engage audiences when meeting and presenting online. A live poll with participants revealed that the hardest part of communicating online is 'not being able to see the reactions of the audience clearly', yet 90% of participants chose to have their cameras off during the workshop.

It's important to listen actively to others when they're speaking in a meeting. It's easy to become complacent about this – especially if you're working from a home office. You may find yourself looking away from the camera or be distracted by an email rather than showing respect to a colleague, stakeholder or client.

 Tip #60 Be a respectful audience in online meetings

Remember that the audience may be able to see you, depending on the speaker/viewer settings they use. It is, therefore, important to be constantly professional, even when you're not actively taking part.

If you wish to appear confident and professional, remember to avoid slouching, walking away from your desk when someone is speaking, eating, checking your phone, touching your face or other distracting body language. Also, remember your facial expressions could be amplified on camera. Expressions such as rolling your eyes, smirking or frowning may not be noticed by most people in a face-to-face meeting, but online, everyone can potentially see you.

If there are other personal reasons why you'd hesitate to have your camera on in your home office, such as privacy reasons, then communicate this to the host in advance. You may also be able to use a virtual background if this works in your home setting.

Where possible, seeing others contributes to more effective communication. It can look odd and feel uncomfortable if cameras are used inconsistently. Seeing audience reactions and reading visual cues are useful strategies and are similar to those you'd use in a face-to-face meeting.

Dress for success: wardrobe Dos and Don'ts

You need to be mindful of what you wear on camera. Some colours and patterns can look distorted or be distracting. Plain colours with subtle patterns are the safest.

Things to avoid wearing on camera include:

- white, strong and bold colours, florals and striped patterns
- long pendants that cut off in the camera frame. Instead, wear something that can be fully in view and isn't so sparkly or bold that it distracts the audience from your face.
- if your filming frame includes the armpits, tops with thin straps can give the impression you're wearing pyjamas or underwear.

You need to dress appropriately for your audience and in line with the purpose of the meeting or presentation or your organisation's image and branding. Working from home doesn't necessarily give you a licence to wear your pyjamas or tracksuit. This is particularly important if you need to stand to give a presentation. When you're sitting, no one can see your Ugg boots. It seems to have become an unspoken protocol for many organisations to have cameras off as the default option, and therefore participants can get away with wearing anything in many instances.

About halfway through a workshop I facilitated recently, I requested all participants turn their cameras on. I was taken by surprise to find that one of the participants was wearing a fluffy pink dressing gown.

Setting up your home 'studio'

Not everybody has the ideal set-up at home with a separate office with plenty of light, adequate space and the flexibility to move furniture and technology around. In fact, some people have to work at the dining table, in their bedroom or in the lounge room. This section will give you some tips on how to make the most of potential limitations in your home office.

One of the most important elements of your home office is where you set up your camera for meetings. Be aware of the light behind you if your camera is facing the window. This can make you look like you're in the dark, create reflection on your face or glasses or make you look pale; all of these will distract your audience and impact your connection with them.

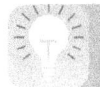 **Tip #61** Consider lighting and background

It's advisable to monitor your privacy and what the audience may see within your camera frame. This is something you should check before the rest of the participants arrive at the meeting. For example, is it appropriate to have a load of washing or dishes behind you or family photos that can be clearly seen? You may need to move your laptop or camera to another place to avoid a distracting backdrop. Some people like to blur the background or place a virtual wall relevant to their business or message. However, if you have a cluttered room, this can affect the quality of your virtual background. You may need to use a green screen for a crisper and more professional quality backdrop.

Where you're seated in relation to your laptop or camera may impact the quality of your relationship with your audience. For example, if your laptop is too low, you'll look like 'Big Brother' looking down at the audience. If your camera is located to the side of your face, you risk losing engagement as the audience will only see your profile and not benefit from your eye contact. If you're in a meeting, this may result in others not acknowledging you or your contributions.

Implementing these simple strategies in your office can be the difference between you being clearly heard and having maximum impact on your audience.

> To help you present with energy, imagine the camera lens is the ideal person you could have in your audience.

On online platforms

Summary of tips for communicating online

Tip #52   Don't use being a technophobe as an excuse.

Tip #53   Be aware of the camera frame.

Tip #54   Look at the camera lens (not the screen).

Tip #55   Encourage active participation.

Tip #56   Stop procrastinating; make a video.

Tip #57   Set the scene for maximum impact.

Tip #58   Be concise with video content.

Tip #59   Set up online meeting protocols.

Tip #60   Be a respectful audience in online meetings.

Tip #61   Consider lighting and background.

9 AT SOCIAL EVENTS

Have you ever been asked to present a speech at a wedding, a 21st birthday, a retirement function, a funeral or other significant event? Were you worried your speech wouldn't be good enough for your friends, family, or colleagues?

This chapter guides you on how to prepare and present a speech worthy of those you love and respect. It covers the broad spectrum of how to include light-hearted humour and heartfelt stories for family and friends at a range of special events. It addresses those moments when you're asked on the spot to give an impromptu speech of recognition, a toast to a colleague or in celebration of an organisational milestone.

Arguably one of the most difficult speeches to deliver is the eulogy. I've included my personal experience of how I managed to maintain my composure when delivering a eulogy for my grandmother, and offer strategies for preparing for these challenging speeches.

Preparing for a special occasion speech

Once you've decided to face your fears and accept the honour of speaking on behalf of family, friends or colleagues, set aside time for your preparation. If your speech is well prepared, you'll feel more secure. Preparation includes deciding on the content and structure of your speech and making time to rehearse and familiarise yourself with the venue.

At social events

Using humour will help you relax, engage your audience, and make the occasion more enjoyable. Start by brainstorming funny memories of the recipient and ask friends and family for their input. Balance your speech by including memorable stories that evoke emotion, thereby illustrating what the recipient means to you.

 Tip #62 Brainstorm light-hearted and heartfelt stories

Be mindful not to include too many 'in-jokes' that only a few people in the audience will understand. To address this, you may need to provide adequate context so everyone can appreciate your stories. The recipients of your speech asked you to speak because of who you are, so remember to be your authentic self and enjoy the opportunity to honour them on their special occasion.

Once you've collected your list of stories, try to create a theme that links the stories together. Doing this will help give your speech logical structure and allow you to narrow down the stories most appropriate for your purpose and support the mood you're trying to create. Three key stories are usually a good number to maintain your audience's interest, and sub-stories can be added if necessary. In his TedxHarding presentation, The Power of Three (2017), Mark Moore discusses the neuroscience behind how audiences feel comfortable with the number three. He explains that the number three is a pattern that humans love because it's familiar, memorable and helps us solve problems. He lists universal and recognisable examples to illustrate how the number three is consistently used in storytelling, in famous speeches and everyday sayings throughout history such as: 'Three Musketeers', 'The Three Little Pigs', 'Friends, Romans, Countrymen', 'Three people walked into a bar ...' and 'Ready, set, go'.

Create a structure with a sequence to help your audience to follow your speech. And if you're nervous about going blank, it will also help you to remember what you planned to say. Under key headings in your notes, include dot points that will trigger your memory.

 Tip #63 Create a structure that's easy for you to remember

Concentrate on memorising the sequence of your speech. So long as you know which part comes next, you don't have to get too caught up in remembering it word for word as losing your place is often what causes problems and anxiety. If you'd like access to a template that demonstrates how to structure a speech for a wedding, which you can adapt for other special occasions, visit: www.completecommunicationcoach.com.au/YDTBH

Create a catchy opening that'll grab the attention of your audience from the beginning. If you can engage your audience within the first thirty seconds, this will help you gain confidence, and your audience will be more likely to be invested in what you present. It's not engaging if you begin by saying something like:

'Hello, my name is Kerry. It's great to be here. Today I'll be speaking about the happy couple.'

Rather, start with a famous quote, a funny anecdote, a poem, a song, a rhetorical question, a story, by showing a prop or by making a thought-provoking statement. After you have their attention, introduce yourself and outline the purpose of your speech if you wish.

Your conclusion is just as important as your opening. It should be memorable and leave your audience with something to think about or close the loop by reminding the audience of where you started. You could use similar strategies as you did for your opening, such as including a quote, a line from a poem, by showing a prop or leaving your audience with a memorable or thought-provoking statement.

Tip #64 Create impact with your opening and conclusion

The final thing you should do once you've finished your conclusion, is smile; if the audience chooses to applaud, stay on stage long enough to acknowledge it, and enjoy it.

Research the venue you'll be presenting in; doing this will help you understand the benefits and limitations of the space. You can visit or phone the venue in advance or look on their website. Some things to consider include:

- Will you be presenting from a raised stage or on the same level as your audience?
- What is the size and shape the room?
- Will you be using a microphone?
- Will there be a lectern or table to put your props or notes on?
- What equipment is available should you wish to include photos or slides?

Standing on a raised platform always assists your audience to see and hear you, no matter where they're sitting. However, if you're standing on the same level as your audience, be mindful of catering to the people sitting or standing at the back, by projecting your voice to the back of the room.

Take the opportunity before the audience arrives to check out your speaking space. Stand in the speaking area so that it's not so foreign to you when it is your turn to get up to speak. Walk around so you know how much room you have and to familiarise yourself. This will help you combat your nerves. You may even have time for a run-through, at least in your head as you move about the stage.

 Tip #65 Research the venue and speaking space

Check the sightlines and make sure any place you intend to present from doesn't obstruct the view for some guests. If using props or other visual aids, work out where you'll place them before and after using them. Position them high enough for everyone to see and make sure they're large enough to be visible. If you intend to include images on screen, ensure your venue has the equipment you need or bring it with you.

If you're not using a microphone, project your voice loudly enough for all the audience to hear. If you're using a microphone, find out what type it is and how to use it. See Chapter 7 for guidelines to follow when using different microphones.

Including humour

If you're going to deliver something humorous, you should believe it's funny so the audience can see that you're comfortable and confident. If you're obviously nervous, the audience may be distracted from laughing out of concern for you. If they can sense that you're relaxed and enjoying your own funny stories, they'll laugh along with you.

At social events

If you can evoke laughter from your audience, there's a good chance they'll be engaged and more open and receptive to hearing your message. Most importantly, relax and have fun.

Tip #66 Have fun using humour in your speech

Try not to look too serious when delivering humour. If your audience laughs, it's okay to laugh along or smile with them – but try not to laugh at your own jokes before the audience laughs. Delivering humour can be easier when presenting to a large audience because laughing is contagious. The more laughter, the better everyone feels and the more evidence you have that you're being successful.

For maximum impact, it's crucial you pause at the right moments and for the right amount of time. There are often two steps when delivering a joke; the set-up and the punchline. It's important to pause at the end of the set-up to build anticipation before delivering the punchline. This leaves the audience hanging, and they'll laugh in relief as they wait for the answer.

If the audience laughs at your jokes, make sure you pause until the laughter subsides before continuing. If you don't, your audience may miss the set-up of the next joke, and of course, if they're laughing loudly, they won't want you to interrupt them too soon.

On the other hand, if the audience doesn't laugh where you expect, don't pause for too long before moving on so that the energy in the room doesn't drop. If you're super-confident, you may be able to make an impromptu joke about the fact that they haven't laughed when they were expected to!

There are some techniques for delivering humour that work well for special occasion speeches that you might like to try.

- Exaggeration: When telling a story, you can embellish it to make it sound sillier. You can also exaggerate your facial expressions, your tone of voice and your gestures.
- Self-deprecation: If you can poke fun at yourself, this can be endearing for your audience but remember that the speech isn't about you. Whatever you include must support the message and stories you're telling about the guest of honour.
- Call back: You may make a joke at the beginning of your speech and then refer to that joke again later in the speech. The familiarity and repetition used creates a community of laughter as everyone collectively recognises your joke.
- Element of surprise: You can surprise the audience with something unexpected. For example, you can use the power of three when telling a joke or story. The third element is totally unrelated to the first and second part, which is what makes it funny. You create a build-up of tension by pausing after the second element and then deliver the unexpected.

Presenting a eulogy

I don't think many people would argue that one of the most challenging presentations is a eulogy for a loved one. It can be tough to keep your emotions at bay to the point where you can get the words out. I've watched people start strongly and then, without warning, lose their composure. That's okay. Some people have to get someone to take over. That's okay too. Hopefully, you're able to say at least some of what you want to say and, if necessary, you can ask someone to finish for you without self-judgement and with loads of self-compassion. If you doubt your ability to prepare and deliver a eulogy, I hope the tips in this chapter help you.

> ### A eulogy for my grandmother
>
> I remember delivering a eulogy for my grandmother. It was one of the hardest things I've ever had to do. But she meant so much to me I wanted to honour her by at least attempting to stay composed. I wore a hat that I had given my grandmother. She was so proud and pleased with this gift that she put on her best dress and new hat and wore them proudly around the house. It was a fun story to tell, which helped to give relief to my story's more moving passages. My cousin stood at the podium with me as I shared this story and the strength and moral support I drew from her was immense. My composure held firm for a while, but at times my emotions took hold. I paused and breathed, and my cousin and I had a backup plan to take over from each other when we needed to. It took a while to get through the eulogy, but I have no regrets.

Telling stories about your loved one are at the heart of your eulogy. Choose stories that represent your memories and are a celebration of the person's life. Collect stories from family and friends so you have moments where you're less emotionally invested when not delivering your own memories.

 **Tip #67** Choose stories for the eulogy carefully

Prepare some funny anecdotes to give some relief and to lighten the moment for you and your audience. Dot these throughout the eulogy, to allow you regular breaks from the sadness.

Develop an uplifting opening and closing rather than an emotional one to help you stay composed. Your audience will benefit from this too.

Decide whether you want to talk directly to your loved one or talk about them. There's no right or wrong way to do it. If your eulogy is for a parent or grandparent, you could choose to use their first name rather than Mum or Pa when you begin the eulogy. This can be relevant when talking about their early life and may help you get through it as it's not quite as personal.

Rehearse your speech over and over until you feel more comfortable. Rehearse in front of friends or family to get some feedback, so you don't experience an emotional reaction for the first time on the day.

Tip #68 Rehearse your eulogy before the funeral

Use your preparation as a grieving tool and release the tears during rehearsal. This may make it easier to manage the emotion in the moment.

On the day of the funeral, treat the speech as an opportunity to celebrate your loved one's life and be proud of yourself for having a go. Be sure to breathe from your diaphragm to relax and help you be in the moment. This will also help with voice projection, which can be compromised when you're feeling emotional.

Tip #69 Manage your emotions on the day

At social events

Wear something special or bring a prop that represents your relationship with your loved one. This may help you feel they're there with you and give you strength in the moment.

If possible, share the responsibility with another family member or friend so you have moral support, and you can hand your notes over if needed.

Delivering a toast or recognition

Being asked to deliver a toast or speech of recognition is commonly thrust upon people in the workplace with little or no warning. Toasts can recognise individuals, multiple people or whole organisations. Examples could include congratulating an employee on their retirement, a significant birthday or farewelling them to a new position. Toasts can also be for recognising milestones or major achievements of an organisation.

If you're put on the spot to give a recognition speech or toast, there are some structures you can follow to help you think on your feet. Following a simple structure can help you avoid waffling and be more memorable and meaningful.

Using 'the power of three' provides a familiar and memorable pattern for audiences. Structuring presentations around the number three is a successfully used formula in many contexts.

 Tip #70 Use a 'power of three' structure for your toast

Along with your 'power of three' structure, you should also be aware of providing a powerful opening to capture your audience's attention and to conclude memorably to leave your audience with something to think about. Adding stories to illustrate these specific outcomes will strengthen the impact of the recognition on the individual and also engage the audience.

Below are three examples of how to use the power of three.

Example 1: Chronological structure recognising contributions over time

When using a 'chronological structure', the aim is to recognise contributions, strengths and qualities demonstrated over time. This is particularly useful when someone is leaving the organisation through retirement or winning a new job.

One: Highlight a notable achievement from when they first started working for the organisation.

Two: Describe more recent or current notable achievements, qualities and contributions made by the employee.

Three: What you envisage for their future and/or what you know they have planned for the future.

By using a chronological approach, you can give recognition to the employee using a story from when they first started at the company. You can follow this with a more recent achievement so the audience can relate. You can conclude by wishing them luck and congratulating them on their next venture.

> **Example 2: Increasing levels of praise**
>
> When using the 'increasing levels of praise' structure, the aim is to start small and get bigger when recognising a colleague at work.
>
> **One:** Recognise the efforts of the individual.
>
> **Two:** Recognise how the individual's efforts have contributed to the success of the organisation.
>
> **Three:** Recognise how this has impacted the world around us.

For example, first focus on the individual's accomplishments by recognising they've had the highest sales for the year. You then move to describe the impact this has had on the organisation, which has increased its exports as a result of this individual's sales efforts. You then get bigger again by pointing out how this individual's efforts have contributed to putting the company on the global market.

> **Example 3: Recognition from broad to specific impact**
>
> The 'recognition from broad to specific impact' structure can be useful when comparing the global and national impact of a project with that of an individual or local organisation. The aim is to start big and then to give recognition to something or someone more specifically.
>
> **One:** Describe the global impact of a project or issue.
>
> **Two:** Describe the national impact of that project or issue.
>
> **Three:** Provide recognition at a local level to an organisation, department or individual.

Starting big and narrowing in on what matters to your specific audience can have a great impact on them, and they'll find themselves able to relate to what is being said. For example, the health minister could talk about how the global pandemic COVID-19 is starting to get under control and how Australia is one of the best performing countries globally. The high praise and recognition can then focus on SA Health who have made South Australia one of the safest places in the world through the efforts of front-line staff, the number of tests that have been undertaken and the quality of the promotions on how to stay safe in our community.

Sometimes, when you provide recognition to a person or organisation, it's appropriate to make a toast. Making a toast is usually done with a celebratory drink such as champagne, if appropriate. To ensure it's a collective gesture of recognition, use a short, simple phrase of three or four words that you say when you raise your glass. This provides a signal to the audience to repeat the phrase when they raise their glasses to toast and recognise the person or organisation. Examples could include: 'To Hannah's new job.', 'To Dimitri's next chapter.' or 'To making our brand global.'

> *An entertaining speech that is worthy of a special occasion includes humorous and heartfelt stories to evoke a range of emotion in your audience.*

Summary of tips for social events

Tip #62   Brainstorm light-hearted and heartfelt stories.

Tip #63   Create a structure that's easy for you to remember.

Tip #64   Create impact with your opening and conclusion.

Tip #65   Research the venue and speaking space.

Tip #66   Have fun using humour in your speech.

Tip #67   Choose stories for the eulogy carefully.

Tip #68   Rehearse your eulogy before the funeral.

Tip #69   Manage your emotions on the day.

Tip #70   Use a 'power of three' structure for your toast.

10 AS AN MC

A Master of Ceremonies, commonly referred to as an MC, is a host and facilitator of an event. The event could be a conference, a social gathering, in the community or at work. This chapter outlines the responsibilities of an MC, along with strategies to be a quality MC.

Responsibilities of the MC

The fundamental responsibilities include to:

- set the tone for the event
- maintain the energy and vibe of the event
- introduce and support the presenters
- manage time
- problem-solve and adjust the program in response to unforeseen circumstances.

As an MC, you're usually the first person an audience sees. You need to start on a high note to set the tone for the event and warm up the crowd, which means connecting with the audience from the start. You can achieve this through effective eye contact, smiling, happy and animated facial expressions and use of humour. Don't forget to introduce yourself and say enough about yourself for the audience to warm to you without upstaging the 'stars of the show'.

 Tip #71 Set the tone

These strategies will help you build a relationship with the audience and create a sense of fun and purpose for the speakers and the audience. Your introduction also sets the scene for the event. Participants expect to hear about housekeeping, such as:

- information about the agenda
- time and duration of scheduled breaks
- the location of toilets, emergency exits, breakout rooms, and other key amenities.

Some of this information may need to be repeated throughout the event to reinforce it for participants.

In addition to communicating effectively with your audience, you need to build a relationship with other players. This could include:

- the speakers
- event organisers
- caterers
- light and sound technicians.

The number of people involved will depend on the nature of the event, the venue and the event management structure. This communication should occur leading up to and on the day of the event.

Tip #72 Build a relationship with event players

Contact each presenter before the event. Request introductions or short biographies (bios) so you know how they want to be introduced. This will allow you to rehearse and be familiar with each speaker and provide you with an opportunity to make sure each speaker knows their allotted time.

It's also important to liaise with technical staff to find out each presenter's audio-visual requirements, microphones and props. Ultimately, it's your job to support 'the stars of the show' to look good.

Arrive early on the day to speak with relevant people, and familiarise yourself with the venue, the presentation space, the lighting, sound, and other equipment such as microphones and lecterns.

Each time you take on the role of MC, treat it as a new and unique experience. Develop an understanding of your audiences so you can target your communication rather than using a one size fits all approach. This may include:

- avoiding unfamiliar terminology, jargon and acronyms
- being aware of industry-specific taboos that may alienate your audience if mentioned
- having a flexible repertoire of jokes and stories suitable for different audiences.

 Tip #73 Tailor communication to different audiences

Do your research about the appropriate dress for the occasion. This will be influenced by who the audience is and the persona that you're aiming to present. If your audience are teenagers at a community event, a corporate uniform is probably not appropriate. If it's a corporate conference, then jeans and a tee-shirt are unlikely to be suitable. If it's a Star Wars event, then don't rock up in a Star Trek costume.

At all events, logistics are going on behind the scenes that the audience will not know about. As MC, remain calm if unexpected events occur and try to keep disruption to a minimum by quickly facilitating a solution. The MC needs to be flexible, problem-solve in the moment, make necessary adjustments to the program, and do it calmly and seamlessly. For example, if the equipment doesn't work for a speaker, the MC can jump in to assist or enlist the assistance of the technical crew if they're available.

Unforeseen circumstances may affect the timings in the program, which will require immediate adjustment. These circumstances could include:

- when a speaker speaks over the allotted time
- an activity that takes longer than expected
- the keynote speaker's flight being delayed
- technical hiccups
- participants returning late from breaks.

Tip #74 Manage time and unforeseen circumstances calmly

The acoustics and size of the venue may affect the sound quality for the MC and other presenters. You should familiarise yourself with the venue before the event, if possible, either by visiting in person, telephoning or looking at the venue website.

If the event is held in a large outdoor or indoor space, microphones are likely to be provided. Research the types of microphones the venue provides as this will impact your performance. If you like to move around the stage and there's only a gooseneck microphone attached to a lectern, you can either request (before the event) a different type of microphone or source one for yourself. Smaller venues may not provide microphones, so being aware of the quality of the venue acoustics and the size of the audience will determine how much you need to project your voice.

On the day of the event, make sure you factor time for sound checks for presenters before the audience arrives. Everyone should feel comfortable and familiar with the equipment.

If presenters wish to use PowerPoint slides or other visual aids, the equipment should be tested and ready to go. You should brief your presenters on this and help them manage the logistics.

Top qualities of an effective MC

To be an effective MC, you need to be well prepared, and rehearsals are vital. Your audience will expect you to appear confident and in control of the program.

An essential starting point is always your vocal quality. It's key to maintaining momentum and interest for the duration of the event. Your aim is to ensure you project your voice appropriately for both the size of the audience and the venue (especially if a microphone isn't available). Speak at a pace that's easy for the audience to keep up; this is likely to be slower than your usual speaking pace.

Tip #75 Maintain engagement through voice and body language

The audience will also benefit if you frequently pause between important points. Pausing gives them time to digest what you've said. Vary the pace, volume, pitch, tone and energy of your voice to maintain interest over a long period. Be sure to warm up your voice to help you sustain its quality for the entire event. See Chapter 4 for detailed information about how to get the best out of your voice.

As an MC

To be a dynamic and confident-looking MC, use open body language. An upright and strong posture, while maintaining a relaxed feel, will contribute to the audience's confidence in you to do your job.

Walk onto the stage with confidence, purpose and energy; move around the stage to engage various parts of the audience. As you stand or sit in the wings waiting for your next transition, be aware of whether the audience can see you. If they can, you need to keep up the energy in how you stand or sit. If they can't see you, by all means, relax, but give yourself time to return to your confident persona before you re-enter the stage. Be ready when a segment has finished to provide seamless transitions.

Remember to:

- smile each time you return
- maintain your enthusiasm and energy
- lead the applause to ensure the speakers get the recognition they'll be hoping for.

Segues can help you transition from one main point to another. These could include words, phrases and sentences that are cues for the audience to move on with you. Similarly, cues or segues between presenters help the program to transition from one segment to another seamlessly. Actively listen to each presenter and be prepared to think on your feet so you can make relevant comments to segue from one speaker to the next.

Tip #76 Use effective tools to support the flow and momentum

You also need to be aware of the peaks and troughs in mood and momentum that occur for audiences. One common trough is after lunch. The audience may return with a stomach full of food, not having finished their conversations, and potentially feeling sluggish and tired from listening. Factoring in energiser activities is a great way to refocus your audience.

Six top qualities of a MASTER of Ceremonies

Maintain energy and momentum

Adapt the program on the spot

Support presenters to be the stars of the show

Test equipment

Engage confidently with the audience

Remain calm

> *An effective MC is flexible, organised, supportive, dynamic and responsive.*

Summary of tips for being an effective MC

Tip #71 Set the tone.

Tip #72 Build relationships with event players.

Tip #73 Tailor communication to different audiences.

Tip #74 Manage time and unforeseen circumstances calmly.

Tip #75 Maintain engagement through voice and body language.

Tip #76 Use effective tools to support the flow and momentum.

11 AT NETWORKING EVENTS

Are you one of the many people who feel uncomfortable at networking events? Or do you struggle to initiate a conversation at the office photocopier? This chapter examines why it can be challenging to talk to strangers, why it can be difficult to put yourself forward, and how to overcome these difficulties.

Why network?

Networking is about building relationships. It's a platform to talk about yourself and your business, to be seen and to meet others who may be potential customers or people who may be able to help you. It's also a way to observe and listen to others so you can collect ideas and strategies for your business. You'll be surprised by the benefits that come to you when you offer support or facilitate a connection between others.

Networking isn't exclusive to attending large business events. You're networking when making casual conversation at the office photocopier or water dispenser, when using social media, making phone calls and speaking with people who you meet in both professional and personal situations. Specific examples of how people network include:

- online communities and chat groups
- volunteering, club, and charity events
- social media
- lunches with former colleagues
- work events and training days

At networking events

- client meetings and phone calls
- leadership initiatives and teamwork activities
- conferences and industry forums
- committee meetings
- happy hours and morning teas.

Confident networkers thrive in networking environments. They have a clear purpose. They pitch themselves and their skills or business with clarity. They know how to make a first impression last. They know how to make themselves heard and how to follow up later.

On the other hand, there are many people with intense fears of networking. I have a colleague who readily delivers speeches and training to large audiences with ease and confidence. However, he is incredibly fearful of networking because he feels uncomfortable initiating conversations. He suffers from imposter syndrome and feels uneasy talking about himself.

When I began writing this chapter, I had my own theories and experiences of networking. To uncover the deep-seated fears that people experience and to explore further strategies for overcoming these fears, I conducted an online survey.

Interestingly, over 40% of survey respondents indicated they enjoyed and valued networking. The survey asked them to provide advice on how to be an effective networker. Their feedback was **GOLD**. I am delighted to share their expertise and strategies with you as we work through concerns and fears of networking.

Tip #77 Face your fears of networking

You may find networking hard the first time you do it, the second, third and maybe even your tenth time, but you'll get better at it the more you put yourself out of your comfort zone. If you persevere, acknowledge your fear and try some strategies in this chapter, your confidence will grow. However, if you avoid such situations, you'll find yourself continually feeding, rather than addressing your fears.

Common fears about networking

If you're reading this, you may be one of the many people who struggle with the idea of networking.

Why is this?

- Is it because you're shy and you find it's easier to be alone?
- Does it stem from your childhood when you were told not to talk to strangers?
- Maybe you don't feel confident initiating conversations?
- Do you think you may be experiencing 'imposter syndrome'? Does this mean you believe no one is interested in listening to you?
- Do you find networking events to be unfriendly environments?

There may be times when your attendance at a networking event is unavoidable. For example, you may find yourself required to attend an industry event. Many people don't feel they have the skills to speak to strangers and feel uncomfortable about approaching others at such events. Some people spend an entire night sitting at the bar hoping the time will pass or that someone

At networking events

will approach them. But, by the end of the evening, they haven't spoken to anyone except the bar staff.

Survey respondents who confessed they don't enjoy networking gave the following reasons:

- social anxiety
- shyness
- feelings of inadequacy
- fear of being judged
- it's exhausting
- it feels fake and contrived
- fear of the unknown
- communicating with strangers
- unconfident selling oneself
- not knowing what to talk about.

Respondents were then asked to rank the most challenging aspects of networking from a prescribed list. The rankings were as follows:

- approaching strangers
- choosing who to approach
- initiating conversations
- keeping a conversation going
- pitching yourself
- feeling that no one would be interested in talking to you
- appearing confident.

> **Quotes from survey respondents**
>
> 'I find it easier to be introduced to someone rather than go up to them and introduce myself. I find it harder to get a natural conversation going other than a few questions, and then it goes quiet.'
>
> 'I never know what to say, so I try to ask the other person questions so that they do all the talking.'
>
> 'I feel nervous and anxious that I might say a stupid thing. I like feeling safe, but then I know it's important, especially for career advancement.'

How to choose who to approach

My clients often say that when they arrive at networking events, they feel overwhelmed by the crowd. They find it difficult to work out who to speak to. They hate the idea of interrupting a conversation, especially when people are huddled in groups. They don't feel confident starting conversations and assume that individuals within these groups don't want to be interrupted. So they avoid them.

Does this sound like you? It might be surprising to realise that others feel just as vulnerable and ill-equipped. Like you, they may be waiting for others to initiate because it's easier for them. In many cases, people will be happy to be interrupted. They're often with their current group because they're comfortable there, not because they're gaining anything from staying in their safety zone.

At networking events

If you don't take the risk, you may miss an opportunity to meet someone who may be able to help you with your work or your business, or who may benefit from your experience.

Tip #78 Be bold – approach who you want to meet

Don't pressure yourself to 'work' the whole room but rather target who you want to speak to. Do some preparation before the event. Find out who is attending by:

- speaking to someone in advance who may have attended a similar event
- contacting the organisers to gather information about who'll be in the audience
- scanning the registration list when you arrive to see some of the organisations represented.

If you have a bit of information on who your audience is, you can prepare yourself. You can decide who you intend to target, what questions you might ask them and how you'll pitch yourself. If there's information you want to give a particular person, make sure it's relevant to their needs, accurate and current.

If you arrive early, the chances are groups will not have formed yet, so it'll be easier to join a group and approach individuals. If you can look beyond your fear, you'll probably notice you're not the only person standing alone, looking awkward and unconfident.

According to survey respondents, you shouldn't assume that others at networking events are 'the enemy' or that they won't be interested in speaking to you, no matter their background or perceived status. They might be very grateful if you rescue them, and it will be empowering for you to do so.

> **Quotes from survey respondents**
>
> 'It's okay to approach people higher on the career ladder than you. Don't let social hierarchy stop you from connecting with others who could be a potential client, mentor or even friend.'
>
> 'Assume friendliness and that people already like you.'

How to approach with confidence

It's important to know how to make a good impression when you meet someone for the first time. This can mean the difference between developing a connection and an influential relationship, or not. Your goal is to appear confident and authentic.

Once you've identified who you want to speak to, observe if they're deep in conversation and assess when you think it would be most appropriate to interrupt or join the conversation.

Then try the following steps to a confident greeting:

- Walk directly and purposefully towards them, so they don't get the impression they're one of many people you want to talk to.
- Use a confident upright posture as you walk.
- When you reach them, give them direct eye contact, a smile and stand square on. If you don't maintain eye contact, or your hips are facing to the left or right, they're likely to miss the cue that you want to speak to them.
- Use open palm gestures to signal you're friendly, approachable and likeable.
- When you're at a comfortable distance, determine whether it's appropriate to extend a handshake.

At networking events

In many western cultures, handshaking is a gesture we commonly use when we first meet someone. It goes a long way in helping to create a lasting first impression.

What does a handshake mean to you? Have you ever been greeted by someone and observed they shake the hand of your colleague but don't offer you the same courtesy? What message did this give you, and what impression did this person make on you?

Have you ever experienced a 'limp fish' handshake? You will know if you have; it's really uncomfortable. It's when a handshake is limp and weak rather than firm and deliberate. When you offer this type of handshake, it leaves the receiver with a poor impression. It can make you appear unconfident or disinterested. On the other hand, if you shake too firmly, you could appear domineering, aggressive, or you may hurt someone. If you seem distracted when handshaking, that is, you look over the shoulder of the receiver or avoid eye contact, you'll risk disconnecting with that person.

> At the time of writing, handshaking was discouraged because of the COVID-19 pandemic.

If handshaking is out of the question, then a smile, eye contact and confident posture will help you create a connection.

If you have a strong belief in your business and what you represent, you will come across as genuine. If you're pretending to be someone you're not, the experience is likely to feel contrived for you and for those you're attempting to meet. However, if you're passionate and care about what you are saying, your audience will care.

Be prepared to ditch the imposter syndrome and realise that people will be interested in meeting and potentially doing business with you. Be prepared to show sincere interest in the people you meet, and they're likely to see you as authentic and trustworthy.

 Tip #79 Be your authentic self

Active listening is the key. Just as you would when delivering a presentation, you need to build rapport and engage with your audience before they'll be prepared to trust what you're saying. Actively listening to the other party will help you maintain the conversation. They're likely to open up to you if you use non-verbal cues that suggest you're genuinely interested in them. This includes:

- maintaining direct eye contact
- smiling
- leaning forward
- directly facing them
- pointing your foot in their direction
- nodding when you agree or understand what they're saying.

These non-verbal cues give the unconscious message that you're tuned in to the conversation.

At networking events

> **Quotes from survey respondents**
>
> 'It's best when it occurs naturally and authentically. Try to generate real interest in other people, which usually isn't that difficult.'
>
> 'Relax so that you can be your authentic self, which will help you connect with people on a personal level. Just go talk to people. You miss every shot you don't take.'
>
> 'It's okay to be yourself in front of strangers … no one's judging you.'
>
> 'Don't pretend to be someone you aren't. By being the real you, you will make the most lasting connections.'
>
> 'I always treat networking as a way of meeting new people. The business end will come naturally, if you're yourself and show genuine interest in the person you're speaking to.'

How to make conversation

When you initiate a conversation, be mindful not to launch immediately into your pitch before breaking the ice. If you don't know the person at all or very well, some small talk about the event, the food, a guest speaker, the venue, or the weather might be a good way to ease into a conversation before you get down to business. Listening will also help you to understand who you are talking to and whether they could be a potential customer worth pitching to.

In her TedxLondon talk, *You Are Contagious, (2017),* Vanessa Van Edwards recommends starting a conversation with questions that influence your audience to 'flip into optimism'. Examples of questions might include: 'Are you working on anything exciting lately?', 'Have you got any holidays coming up?' or 'Anything exciting happen today?'

> **Tip #80** Ask questions that encourage positive conversation

Asking this type of question will make you more memorable as you've asked your audience to share information that makes them feel positive. On the flip side, if you start a conversation with, 'Have you been busy lately?', 'What do you do?' – these types of questions may not prompt happy responses and may have the opposite effect. They'll not help you build and maintain a positive conversation and rapport.

Prepare some generic open questions you can ask if there are moments of awkward silence. If you use closed questions that require a single word answer like yes or no, it will be more difficult to maintain the conversation. For example, 'Have you attended one of these events before?' could be better phrased as, 'How good do you think this event is compared to others you have been to?'

Networking is a two-way street. Whilst it's important to ask questions to determine whether it's worth pitching your products or services, it's equally important to see if you can assist others. Offering to connect them with someone you know is a great way to do this.

> **Tip #81** Look for opportunities to assist others

At networking events

If you help others, they're more likely to remember you and recommend you in the future. You may not see immediate rewards, but you might be surprised by what comes your way.

Networking is about gradually building connections. It is important to be strategic when networking. It is not about getting business every time. It is about meeting people, building rapport and being memorable. If you come on too strong, you are likely to put people off. Let them get to know you first. Building trust is what helps you to sell. If you create a positive impression, then others will remember you the next time they see you. Or when they need a product or service like yours, they are more likely to get in touch with you.

Here's an example of how this has worked for me at a networking event.

MY NETWORKING STORY

I attended an event last year where I didn't know anybody. I headed straight for the coffee line and struck up a conversation with the person in front of me. I saw her at another event and as she was a familiar face, I approached her again. We chatted further and she introduced me to some other people. Three months later, she sent me an email saying:

'Ever since the day I met you in the coffee line I have imagined working with you. Fast forward, this week I have been asked to be a keynote speaker at a function. I am excited but nervous. I would love to have a session with you to help me prepare.' (Anonymous 2021)

Creating an elevator pitch

An elevator pitch is essentially a 30-second to 1-minute story about who you are and what you do. It's appropriately named for those moments when you need to quickly attract someone's attention and leave a positive impression before either of you 'leaves the elevator' or moves on. The aim is to access more time with this person based on their in-the-moment impression and reaction. At a networking event, when you think that someone you want to meet may have limited time, aim to deliver a short pitch to get their attention and influence them to want to speak with you further.

It's worth creating different versions of your pitch that vary in length to use in a variety of circumstances. These could include 1 to 2 minutes, 5 minutes, or even longer if you can pitch as part of a presentation. The key to creating an authentic and attractive pitch is to have a clear understanding of what you do and what you represent and value. The level of detail you include will depend on the circumstances.

Some questions you can ask yourself when creating your pitch:

- What's your goal in communicating with your audience?
- What do they need to know about you?
- How much time do you have to pitch yourself or your products and services?
- How will you communicate this with confidence?
- What's the message or takeaway for your audience?

At networking events

Elevator pitches at networking events need to be succinct, as you may be interrupted and only have a small window to deliver them. One possible structure uses the power of three which was discussed in Chapter 9. For example,

One: Introduce yourself using a few personal details, e.g. your name, the organisation you represent, your role and pain points of your customers.

Two: Explain what you can do for them, what you believe in, what you are passionate about, why you are at this event, how you can solve problems of your customers.

Three: Include stories. The length of your pitch will determine how much time you can spend telling stories relevant to the problems you solve. Stories will make you more memorable and are likely to influence your audience to continue the conversation.

Remember, when you approach someone, they may have heard many pitches already. To ensure you're heard, deliver yours with passion and sincerity.

Tip #82 Prepare an elevator pitch and deliver with passion

Use confident and open body language so that you can build a trusting relationship and a powerful connection. An audience will know if you're not authentic. Let them see the real you, show them why your pitch matters to you and how it should matter to them. This will help you encourage the continuation of the conversation as you ignite your audience's curiosity and interest.

What do you fear more – networking or presentations?

I asked the survey question: Would you prefer to attend a networking event for a hundred people or to present to a hundred people?

It intrigued me to discover that there was an even divide for one option or the other. Only a small number indicated that they equally enjoy networking and public speaking, as both provide opportunities for connecting with people. A small number admitted that both options are unattractive to them:

> **Quotes from survey respondents**
>
> 'I find the thought of presenting to a hundred people or being in a room full of strangers at a networking environment equally terrifying.'
>
> 'Well, I'm not any good at speaking to a large group of people I do not know. So I'd much rather just be there but not speak.'

Why do some people prefer presenting over networking?

Some survey respondents revealed that presenting is easier because you can prepare and rehearse in advance. Many also have the mindset that the audience has chosen to attend a presentation to listen to you, but they may not choose to readily speak to you at a networking event. When networking, you're required to think on your feet, which can be nerve-wracking.

The other reason highlighted by respondents was that giving a presentation breaks the ice. The audience has learnt something about you, which may encourage them to approach you, wanting to find out more. This takes the pressure off having to make connections when networking.

> **Quotes from survey respondents**
>
> 'As a speaker, you can present your subject or idea and have people understand you or your product. If people want to know more, they'll come and connect with you. In short, it breaks the ice.'
>
> 'People will more likely start a conversation with you if they feel like they know you already.'

Why do some people prefer networking over presenting?

Many consider networking easier because if things go wrong, it's easier to retreat. After all, you're not the centre of attention. If things aren't going well for you, it's likely nobody will know except you. There's also the potential to find others in a room who are just as apprehensive as you are when networking, so you're not alone like you often are when giving a presentation.

These people experience less fear when networking compared with presenting because they can avoid putting themselves out of their comfort zones and they're not the centre of attention. However, if you are not willing to participate, you will gain little benefit from attending such events.

> **CLIENT STORY: Exceptional networker fears presenting**
>
> I have coached a businesswoman, whose success is predominantly due to her networking ability. During one of our coaching sessions, she told me that networking is easy for her because she knows herself and her core values so well. She feels comfortable talking about herself. However, she doesn't feel the same level of confidence when delivering prepared presentations; in fact, she has an intense fear of speaking in front of a group and avoids it at all costs.
>
> My job as her coach was to show her that many of her networking skills are transferable to presenting. She feels comfortable talking about herself, so she can tell her story as the key part of a presentation. When networking, she presents herself with energy and enthusiasm; she can also engage a big audience with the same skills when presenting. She builds relationships by being authentic and passionate, which are wonderful qualities for a presenter. She confidently thinks on her feet when asked impromptu questions at a networking event. She can use the same skills if something doesn't go to plan when giving a presentation.
>
> It's all about mindset and recognising you can communicate confidently in any situation if you have self-belief and strategies for controlling your fears.

Follow up

Your networking doesn't stop once you leave an event. You may have exchanged business cards or details and planned to get in touch. You need to follow up if you feel you've built a connection and a potential ongoing relationship with someone. Don't wait for them to contact you. Email them first if that seems easier. Let them know you enjoyed meeting them and that you'll be contacting them. Invite them to meet with you face to face to continue to build your relationship. Suggest meeting for a coffee.

At networking events

Telephone or video calls are other forms of networking, and while talking face to face is more effective, this is not always possible as they might be interstate or overseas.

 Tip #83 Follow up after networking events

Opportunities will pass you by if you wait for someone to contact you. Be proactive. Be confident in what you offer.

> **Quote from survey respondent**
>
> 'Act upon networking advice or connections that you make. Don't just network.'

Informal networking

Casual conversations at the office water cooler or photocopier can be an effective form of networking. Some people believe that if they work hard and don't waste time chatting at work, their hard work and dedication will be noticed and rewarded. Big mistake! While you're quietly buried at your desk, your colleagues are developing relationships through casual conversations, making them more memorable and noticeable.

I've worked with clients who find it hard to start conversations at work if they don't know their colleagues very well. Listen to what others are saying when you're waiting for your turn at the water cooler. You might pick up something you can use as a conversation starter at another time. For example, they might love talking about their pet, their children or their hobbies.

You can also note what matters to a colleague by what they share in meetings. Better still, be a little early to meetings and chat with colleagues who are already there. Use this as a hook to start a conversation when you next run into them. You can talk about the traffic or the weather or a current news item; easy topics that everyone can comment on.

 Tip #84 Listen for conversation starters

As you get to know someone, it'll be easier the next time you run into them. If they say something to you, be sure to give them direct eye contact, a smile and use open body language so they can see you're approachable and have a genuine interest in what they're saying. They're more likely to respond to you positively, as you've made an effort to develop a trusting relationship. The time you spend informally developing relationships and building trust will help you to influence them in a more formal meeting or when working together.

Similarly at a networking event, take opportunities to speak with strangers in the coffee or registration queue or at your table. Listen to what they have to say so you can determine if you would like to speak with them later at the event. Once you have made this informal connection, it makes it easier to approach them during a break and to potentially pitch your services or products to them, if relevant.

> *Networking is about gradually building connections; not about rushing in to deliver your pitch.*

Summary of tips for effective networking

Tip #77   Face your fears of networking.

Tip #78   Be bold – approach who you want to meet.

Tip #79   Be your authentic self.

Tip #80   Ask questions that encourage positive conversation.

Tip #81   Look for opportunities to assist others.

Tip #82   Prepare an elevator pitch and deliver with passion.

Tip #83   Follow up after networking events.

Tip #84   Listen and observe colleagues to gather conversation starters.

12 AS A TECHNICAL PRESENTER

Have you ever struggled to present technical information to an audience outside of your field? Have you ever had to synthesise years of research into a short presentation that's suitable for different audiences?

Communicating specialist language

Presenting technical and specialist information to a non-technical audience can be tough if you're not accustomed to it. This is common in industries such as engineering, science, information technology, finance, the medical industry or trades. You need to adopt the mindset that your audience may be uninformed about your topic, rather than assuming they'll never understand because they're stupid.

Specialist fields are riddled with discipline-specific jargon, acronyms and terminology. As industries evolve and become increasingly more specialised, so does the language. You may not even know you're speaking jargon because it becomes part of your everyday language. Your challenge is to make complex topics accessible to a lay person by using language that everyone knows whilst also honouring your field. You'll need to work out how to define technical terms in everyday language.

If you present the same information to all audiences, you'll not be successful in educating the community. The level and amount of information you share as well as the language you use should vary from audience to audience. For example, if you are a scientist it would be unwise to deliver the same presentation to a group of peers as you would to a school or community group. Ask questions before and during your presentation to gather information about your audience. Don't assume what people know about your topic; find out the knowledge level and background of your audience and tailor your subject matter accordingly. In some cases, you may need to break it down into accessible and easy-to-digest chunks.

 Tip #85 Tailor your content for different audiences

In *WIRED* magazine (2017), Neuroscientist Bobby Kasthuri explains scientists need to educate people about the benefits of science beyond their field. You can quickly help people understand and be fascinated by new concepts and ideas if you tailor your communication to different audiences. Kasthuri demonstrated this by describing the benefits of a neuroscience concept, 'connectome', to five different audiences:

- a 5-year-old
- a teenager
- a science student from a different science discipline
- a neuroscience graduate student
- a connectome entrepreneur.

Bobby Kasthuri asked questions of each of the above audiences to gauge their level of knowledge. He then tailored the complexity of his language and concepts for each audience. For example, he started by asking the five-year-old if he understood what a brain is, whereas he asked the science student if she understood the term 'connectome'. To engage the five-year-old, he used analogies that the child could understand. For example, he compared the number of cells in the brain to the number of stars in the sky, which quickly sparked the young person's imagination and curiosity. Adults also engage when they feel curious and are encouraged to use their imagination.

Tip #86 Ask questions and use analogies to spark curiosity and imagination

He used different examples that the teenager could relate to and increased the level of complexity. With the science student, he could use scientific terms but not necessarily those specific to neuroscience. He could tap into the neuroscience student's specialist expertise, knowing that she was familiar with and understood some of the terminologies. Finally, when talking to the connectome entrepreneur, he communicated in a conversational style to encourage him to share his ideas and expertise. He quickly covered a lot of ground, whereas, with the other audiences, he walked them through more slowly to ensure they understood.

Kasthuri demonstrated you don't have to eliminate jargon completely. But you need to be aware that you're using it in the first place. You can explain it in a way that's accessible and easy to understand. He used the word 'connectome' with each person and explained the term in a way that they each could understand, enabling him to create awareness and honour an important scientific concept.

Tip #87 Use everyday language rather than jargon

The next time you communicate your specialist knowledge to a non-specialist audience, undertake an audience analysis before presenting so the information can be tailored appropriately.

As a technical presenter

Remember to think from the audience's perspective, not from yours. Consider their knowledge levels, their demographic backgrounds and their reasons for being there.

Identifying the message

After you've determined your audience's background and knowledge, you need to choose content that will matter to your specific audience. You can't share everything, so you'll need to determine the message or actions you want your audience to adopt.

Sharing research or information about a project that has taken you years to complete usually means you're completely invested in it. If you just present the findings and recommendations without outlining their importance and relevance to your audience, they'll probably find it boring.

Research that's written is often not suitable for a verbal presentation. Don't insult your audience by reading your research to them, but rather communicate important areas of interest in short, crisp sentences.

All your content should support your message. Can you state it in a single sentence or two? Prepare to cull any content from your presentation that doesn't support your message.

Tip #88 Create content and structure that ensures a clear message

Often the general purpose of a technical presentation is to inform or educate an audience, and sometimes to persuade them to act. This may include presenting a proposal where you want to advocate for a product, service, design, project, or idea.

Important elements of persuasive presentations, which may form the foundation for your basic structure, include:

- gaining the attention and curiosity of the audience (using a lay statement)
- presenting problems and feasible solutions
- helping the audience to imagine the solutions
- persuading the audience to act.

Be specific about what you want the audience to do. Don't leave it vague. Convince them to take action by explaining the relevance and significance in clear and simple terms.

The order of your presentation is important to ensure your message is clear. Make time to rehearse your speech. You may need to practice out loud to ensure you haven't left some information too late in your presentation for the audience to follow your thread. When structuring your speech, developing a flow diagram may help you see the logical connections between each part of your speech. Seek feedback when rehearsing to ensure the sequence of information helps the audience understand the topic and message in logical steps.

Make your presentation easy to follow, by:

- organising it in a logical structure
- including an introduction, body and conclusion
- including segues as signposts to help audiences transition from one point to another
- communicating your message early in the speech
- restating the message later to emphasise its importance and to ensure the audience remembers.

Keeping your audience engaged

Have you ever seen a presenter read their research notes to the audience? This can show limited preparation and confidence and leave the audience feeling uninspired.

Consider gaining the audience's interest from the start by challenging them to think outside the box. Encourage them to invest in your topic by demonstrating why it should matter to them and how it relates to them. Use examples, analogies and stories to engage their curiosity and imagination, to help build rapport and make it memorable. Stories about the origins of your project or the history of how theories and developments have changed over time are great examples to share.

The more opportunities you take to change it up, shift the momentum, move the focus, or alter the pace, the more engaged your audience will be. This can be achieved by including activities where participants can be actively involved, challenged and can interact and problem solve with each other.

Tip #89 Include activities to maintain interest

You can also offer a range of opportunities for interaction to encourage active participation rather than listening passively. These could include:

- facilitating group activities
- launching live polls
- question-and-answer or panel sessions
- standing to interact with others in the room
- providing a question or problem to discuss e.g. a scenario to predict an outcome.

If you notice interest waning, it may also be a result of your delivery. You can change the volume, pitch and pace of your voice or move to a different part of the room to regain attention.

You owe it to your audience to undertake sufficient preparation and rehearsal to make sure you deliver in a lively, animated and enthusiastic way. Being authentic and showing your passion for your field will help your audience relate to you, trust you and to become excited about your topic.

Tip #90 Demonstrate passion for your topic

Kasthuri (2017) used animated body language to inspire and engage his audiences. He showed enthusiasm and excitement for his topic, which had a contagious impact on his audiences. For example, he:

- sat forward in an engaging and inviting way
- used direct eye contact and smiled
- used animated and excited facial expressions
- showed he was actively listening through nodding and making each person feel comfortable and validated
- mirrored the body language of the entrepreneur to show respectfully that they were on the same level.

Nailing a Q&A session

Often technical presentations include question-and-answer (Q&A) sessions. As a speaker, these sessions can be beneficial to you because you can:

- determine if the audience has understood the technical content and your message
- gauge whether a proposal has been supported

- address concerns that may impact audience acceptance
- showcase your technical knowledge.

Some speakers are happy to take questions throughout a presentation, which helps them determine whether the audience has understood the content as they go along. Be mindful, though, as this can be disruptive to your presentation flow, and often questions are naturally answered as you progress through your content. Most commonly, presenters advise the audience that there will be time to ask questions at the end. Ensure you keep this promise by allowing buffer time for this purpose.

Being in control of the Q&A session is paramount to ensure it runs smoothly and on time. For some events, another person may run the Q&A. To ensure your expectations are met, communicate with them prior to the presentation.

Authoritative body language should be used to direct the order of questions, almost like a traffic officer, so the audience is clear which questions will be answered first, second, third, and which ones will be answered after the event.

Tip #91 Take control of your Q&A session

Be aware that your presentation may provoke too many questions or no questions at all, depending on your topic and audience dynamics. You need to be prepared for both scenarios. Have something organised in case there are no questions. This could be information you wanted to share but didn't expect to have the time to include. You could also use the time to propose questions to your audience.

If you receive many questions, it's important not to go overtime. Be prepared to keep your answers short and succinct. It's disrespectful to your audience to spend the entire question time on one question. If someone tries to ask a multifaceted question, politely interrupt them and offer to answer the first part. Invite them to discuss the other parts in the break or to follow up after the event.

You might be one of the many people who fear thinking on their feet and who find it difficult to respond to questions confidently.

Tackling impromptu speaking is all about mindset. You can't possibly know everything about your topic. So give yourself a break and realise this doesn't make you less of an expert. How you respond to not knowing is much more important than the not knowing.

 Tip #92 You don't need to have all the answers

Confidently and assertively say that you don't know and promise to find out. Or ask if anyone else in the audience knows the answer, so you take the attention away from you. Above all, don't pretend you know, as this will impact your credibility.

It's not necessary to answer an impromptu question immediately. If you rattle off the first thing that comes into your head, you risk looking as if you're regurgitating something you've pre-prepared rather than giving the question the thought it deserves. If you need time to think about an answer, you can invite the person to catch up with you one on one later. Or something might come to you after you've answered some other questions.

If you need a small amount of time to think, you can buy yourself that time by trying strategies such as:

- pausing and breathing to centre yourself and remain calm
- repeating or paraphrasing the question
- repeating your primary message and weaving in an answer to support your message.

You'll kick yourself if you respond too quickly. Often, you'll think of something once you've had time to think, so take a moment and your mind will respond more effectively.

 Tip #93 Pause to allow time to think about your answer

Another important aspect of managing a Q&A session involves dealing with difficult audience members. Avoid being defensive if someone appears to want to discredit you, or to be disruptive, or if they seem to want to dominate the conversation. Welcome their questions but be polite, assertive and calm. If their questions don't support the scope of your presentation, cut them short and offer to catch up with them one on one to discuss further.

You can anticipate and prepare for questions that may be asked. You can rehearse your presentation in front of colleagues to help identify some of the questions that might be raised. You can then rehearse succinct answers to these questions.

Allow time to summarise your presentation after question time to ensure you're in control of how you leave your audience. Conclude by reinforcing your message or call to action.

Visual aids for technical content

Some people use models as visual aids. These are useful to help audiences grasp complex concepts and make them easier to explain. Even in everyday situations such as a medical appointment, the practitioner may bring out a skeleton to present visually what they're trying to explain. This saves the practitioner or presenter from describing what something looks like and creates a more engaging and easy-to-understand experience.

 Tip #94 Visual aids should support understanding

If you use tools such as PowerPoint and Prezi, they should support rather than dominate your presentation. Your audience is there to see you and listen to you, not read your slides. Include moments where you black out your screen and talk freely and directly with the focus on you.

If you choose to use visual aids for your presentations, they should be:

- ♦ easy to understand
- ♦ engaging
- ♦ easy to see from the back row of the audience
- ♦ supportive of your purpose and message.

See Chapter 7 on presentations for detailed information on how to present effectively with visual aids.

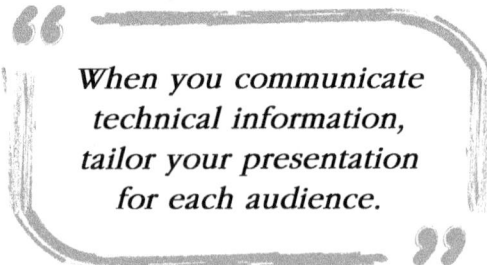

When you communicate technical information, tailor your presentation for each audience.

Summary of tips for communicating technical content

Tip #85 Tailor your content for different audiences.

Tip #86 Ask questions and use analogies to spark curiosity and imagination.

Tip #87 Use everyday language rather than jargon.

Tip #88 Create content and structure that ensures your message is clear.

Tip #89 Include activities to maintain interest.

Tip #90 Demonstrate passion for your topic.

Tip #91 Take control of your Q&A session.

Tip #92 You don't need to have all the answers.

Tip #93 Pause to allow time to think about your answer.

Tip #94 Visual aids should support, not dominate, your technical presentation.

13 AS A LEADER

The qualities covered in Chapters 1 to 12 will help you communicate effectively to be an inspirational and influential leader. These qualities include your ability to:

- exude confidence
- create connections
- be authentic and trustworthy
- use effective body language
- read and respond to the non-verbal cues of others
- manage meetings
- think on your feet
- deliver confident face-to-face and online presentations
- influence audiences
- engage and maintain engagement of audiences
- be an active listener
- be an effective networker
- explain specialist, technical and complex concepts to audiences outside your field.

This chapter focuses on the most important communication strategies and skills that will help make you an inspirational and influential leader.

Sharing what's important to you

If you want to bring others along for the ride, be prepared to communicate regularly with your team in a clear, passionate, and transparent way, so they understand what's important to you and why their work matters.

As a leader

In his book *How Great Leaders Inspire Everyone To Take Action* (2011), Simon Sinek explains that leaders who inspire always start with 'the why'; their vision or purpose.

Tip #95 Communicate your vision – emphasise the 'why'

Sinek proposes that most leaders know what they do; some know how they do it, but few can articulate why they do it. He says that all the great and inspiring leaders throughout history think, act and communicate in the same way. To demonstrate this, he uses what he refers to as his Golden Circle. The Golden Circle shows successful leaders start from the centre of the circle with 'the why', and then work their way to the outer circles to expand on 'the what' and 'the how'.

The benefits of starting with 'the why' are scientifically proven through neuroscience. When you communicate from the inside out, you're tapping into the limbic brain which is responsible for feelings (such as trust and loyalty). This allows you to influence and impact the behaviour and decision-making of others. Talk about your beliefs and vision if you want to attract others who believe what you believe.

Sinek emphasises that making a profit isn't a vision but rather a result of the vision. Leaders miss the mark if they try to motivate their teams by focussing on monetary outcomes only.

Sinek uses Martin Luther King as an example of a leader who knew how to communicate his vision, his why and his beliefs. People whose vision resonated with his were motivated to share it, and so Luther King's vision was widely spread. Have you ever wondered why Martin Luther King's famous speech was 'I have a dream' and not 'I have a plan'?

There may be some people on your team, or even other leaders, who are disengaged from your vision. You may notice they don't actively involve themselves in meetings, or they may seem to block your vision. To motivate them to be in sync with you, and to understand their concerns, you may need to start a conversation. Speaking to them individually can allow you to understand any issues better and resolve potential conflict. Specific strategies could include to:

- make a special effort to engage with them individually
- give them important tasks
- liaise with them about an important issue
- ask them what they're interested in doing, and work together to develop a way for them to pursue their interests
- ensure they feel valued.

Choose an appropriate time to chat with your team member. Conversations of this nature can sometimes be challenging, and you should avoid the risk of either party becoming defensive. You might find that your team member is interested in being more engaged, but they may feel devalued, or may not understand your vision. Perhaps they feel they're not making a meaningful contribution, so they withdraw. Their disengagement may also not be work-related but rather due to personal reasons. If this is the case, be respectful of their privacy and what they feel comfortable sharing with you.

Use your communication skills to uncover the reasons behind their disengagement and work together to identify strategies to resolve their concerns.

 Tip #96 Engage with disengaged colleagues with an open mind

As a leader

If you avoid proactively tackling what you may perceive as their resistance, this may impact the culture of your team and your business, which will make it harder for you to fulfil your vision. Most importantly, determine whether they understand and believe in your vision.

In 2019, I attended a workshop on inspirational leadership facilitated by Ben Waldon, a leadership trainer and Artistic Director of a business called Contender Charlie. Waldon's key messages mirrored those of Simon Sinek's theory on 'the why'. Waldon used the story of King Henry V of England to illustrate inspirational leadership qualities. He suggested that Henry V was an effective leader because he modelled what he stood for and influenced his followers to envisage and to live 'the why'. To coin an old phrase, Henry V 'practised what he preached'. If your team isn't on board with you, it's probably because your vision isn't clear to them.

Tip #97 Model the behaviour that you value

Henry V had great success as a leader as he was committed to what Waldon refers to as 'syncing the tribe'. By communicating and demonstrating 'the why', he was able to nurture a common identity for his team. Everyone was working towards the same goal. His motto was: 'We are in this together'. Leaders who articulate and live their vision are seen as innovative because they think ahead and motivate others with possibilities.

Be prepared to communicate your vision with energy and passion to ignite enthusiasm in others. You can achieve this by being animated when you speak and showing enthusiasm through your voice and body language. For example, don't be afraid to show your excitement about something by smiling, being wide-eyed and using animated gestures, as this will be contagious for your listeners. If you speak in a monotone voice, frown, lack energy and avoid eye contact, it'll have a very different effect. Your audience is less likely to be engaged when you speak, trust you or be enthusiastic about your leadership.

Tip #98 Be passionate

When someone presents their beliefs with passion, they tend to be dynamic, and it's difficult not to be drawn to them. Approach team members with upright body language to demonstrate you are confident; don't give others any reason to doubt the importance and authenticity of your vision.

Stories are powerful. Show your vulnerability by sharing stories about yourself and others. Anyone can share facts, figures and information, but sharing stories that support these, will enable you to influence hearts and minds. Relevant stories that include images, metaphors and analogies will engage and enthuse your audience and illustrate why something matters to you and your audience. People will remember your stories for years to come because they allow you to tap into their emotions.

Tip #99 Influence hearts as well as minds

Showing vulnerability helps you to develop trust and encourages others to share their stories with you. Not all stories need to be emotionally charged. A humorous story can be equally powerful. If it evokes a smile, laughter, or joy, it'll help you and your audience relax. You're likely to be more approachable. People will feel comfortable with you if you're not business-like and serious all the time.

Valuing your team

If you want your team to be loyal and in sync with your vision, they need to know that you value their input, skills, and contribution. Demonstrate that you value them as individuals and listen actively to their needs, concerns, and ideas.

Don't assume they know you appreciate them. Tell them specifically, both formally in performance appraisals and informally, in the moment, when they impress you. Be honest, open and transparent. You may believe that a colleague is performing well and assume they know what you think. If you don't provide regular feedback, some people may feel ignored, excluded or vulnerable. This can lead to disengagement or reduced motivation, confidence and productivity.

Some leaders deliberately don't disclose or share information with their team – this is often obvious and can lead to mistrust. Those who don't feel valued and who don't trust you, are not likely to go that extra mile to support your vision.

There is a vast chasm between leaders who just listen and those who actively listen. Some people describe this as being mindful. If you want to connect, influence and have your voice heard, it's important to concentrate on being fully present, in the moment and not distracted by other things or thoughts. When you're actively listening, you'll make your audience feel valued and they are more likely to be open with you.

 Tip #100 Listen actively

YOU DESERVE TO BE HEARD

Even the busiest of leaders need to put time aside to listen intently. This means focussing completely on the people you're communicating with rather than having your head elsewhere due to competing priorities. You're better off rescheduling a meeting with your team members than not giving them the time and attention they deserve.

Sometimes team members may just want to be heard, so don't interrupt them unless the conversation is counterproductive. If you pre-empt what somebody is saying, they may not trust you and may not be open with you in the future. Be prepared to show your team that you have listened, through your actions. They will respect you more if you don't always dig your heels in and insist on doing things your way but are prepared to change in response to their input.

It's important to give non-verbal cues that will make your audience feel heard and to show them you value the time you spend with them. Greet them with a smile and ensure you make direct eye contact. Use open palm gestures as you invite them into your office, or when you're explaining something. Use subtle cues, such as nodding to show you agree or you understand what someone is telling you.

If you avoid eye contact, this can cause your audience to:

- mistrust you
- feel uncomfortable
- think you're hiding something
- anticipate that you intend to deliver bad news.

As a leader

Be aware of distracting body language, such as looking up when thinking, clasping hands, playing with jewellery, putting hands in pockets or rocking on feet, as this may cause disconnect and lack of trust.

> **Quotes from workshop participants**
>
> 'Listening to teammates can get the job done faster; it'll help the person who is talking feel valued so that they won't give up.'
>
> 'Active listening enables me to appreciate situations and problems more. As a result, I can answer questions in an organised way and gain more information and understanding.'
>
> 'It was amazing to learn about active listening and how it affects the person talking.'

As a successful leader, you'll need to adapt your communication for a variety of audiences and purposes. You need to understand each individual in your team, their communication and learning style, strengths, values and background. This will enable you to tailor what you say and how you say it.

Tip #101 Adapt your communication for different team members

Tune in to the non-verbal cues of others. Do they appear nervous and need to be put at ease? Do they look angry and need to be listened to without interruption? Are they bursting with enthusiasm to share an idea?

Reading the signs will help you tailor what you say and how you say it. You may need to adapt the language you use and the information you share to help your audience understand.

Or you may need to adjust your tone of voice to make the person feel comfortable. If you're unsure, ask questions. Be prepared to adapt your communication, be inclusive, and demonstrate that you value difference.

You deserve to be heard, and so do they.

> *Leaders who start with 'the why', or their vision, will inspire and motivate their teams and engender trust and loyalty.*

As a leader

Summary of tips for leaders

Tip #95 Communicate your vision – emphasise 'the why'.

Tip #96 Engage with disengaged colleagues with an open mind.

Tip #97 Model the behaviour that you value.

Tip #98 Be passionate.

Tip #99 Influence hearts as well as minds.

Tip #100 Listen actively.

Tip #101 Adapt your communication for different team members.

CONCLUSION

Research suggests that up to 75% of people struggle with a genuine fear of public speaking.

If you're one of these people, I'm guessing you miss out on opportunities because you don't feel confident to put yourself forward. You don't share your ideas and stories because you don't believe you deserve to be heard.

You aren't alone, but it doesn't need to be this way. Even some of the most clever, talented and driven people face these challenges. I urge you to start by facing and acknowledging your fear. Yes, this will mean you will need to put yourself out of your comfort zone, but the more you do it, the more chance you have for success. It will get better.

I've written my book in the hope it will reach as many people as possible who experience this fear. Included are lots of easy-to-apply strategies you can use in a range of both personal and business situations that will help you feel more empowered.

Start by breathing, adopting confident body language and visualising success.

For more support or help, work with a trusted friend, colleague, or a public speaking coach. Ask them to watch you present, observe you in meetings, take you through a mock interview and give you feedback. Or, if you want information on any of the topics covered in my book, visit my website for a list of free resources, cheat sheets and templates that

CONCLUSION

will support your communication in a range of situations: www.completecommunicationcoach.com.au/YDTBH

Please take confidence and hope from the stories in this book. There are people just like you who thought they couldn't do it, who were terrified of failure, of being judged or of freezing up. But they courageously broke through this and have seen enormous success.

They, like you, deserve to be heard.

ACKNOWLEDGEMENTS

I have many people to thank for helping me to fulfil the dream of writing my book.

A big thank you to my coach and friend, Darrell Klar, for picking me up when I've doubted myself and for teaching me how to follow my dreams and recognise my strengths. I wouldn't have gone into business without you.

To my editors, Joanne Speirs from Nurturing Words and my dear friends, Karen Hill and Marianne Hammat, thank you for helping me to lift the words off the page in a dynamic and logical way.

To my many clients who've allowed me to include their stories and testimonials in this book, I owe you a huge debt of gratitude.

Thank you to the amazing Toastmaster community for supporting me to become an effective public speaker and coach. In particular,

- Joanne Kneebone for working with me to create a workshop for communicating online, and her many other hours of support.
- Nick Kastelein for sharing his knowledge about how to communicate technical content and for partnering with me to write *A Toastmasters Guide to Speech Evaluation*.
- Bob Stanford and Johnny Rizk for their generosity and talent to provide photographs and images.

Acknowledgements

To my niece, Sarah, and friend, Tanya, thank you for your artistic input.

To my sister, Kathryn, for all of her advice and support, and especially for introducing me to the 'Read Aloud' tool on Microsoft Word – it was a game changer!

To my husband, Leonard, and son, Oliver, thank you for your daily support and love. To my mum and dad, thanks for encouraging me to challenge myself and try new things outside of my comfort zone.

To my dear friends who brainstormed with me on a weekend away over a glass of wine, all the scenarios where one deserves to be heard – I heard you!

BIBLIOGRAPHY

Barnes Kim B (2015) *Exercising Influence: A Guide for Making Things Happen at Work, at Home, and in Your Community*, John Wiley & Sons, Third Edition.

Bodycoat M (2019) *Voice workshop, Speechmatters.*

Bosworth MT and Zoldan B (2012) *What Great Salespeople Do: The Science of Selling Through Emotional Connection and the Power of Story*, McGraw-Hill, New York.

Cuddy, A. J. C., Wilmuth, C. A., Yap, A. J., & Carney, D. R. (2015) *Preparatory power posing affects nonverbal presence and job interview performance.* Journal of Applied Psychology, 100(4), 1286–1295.

Cuddy A (2 October 2012) '*Your Body Language May Shape Who You Are*', https://www.ted.com/talks/amy_cuddy_your_body_language_may_shape_who_you_are?language=en, accessed 13 April 2020.

Gilbert E (2016) *Big Magic*, Bloomsbury Publishing PLC.

Hettiarachchi D (2015) *Masterclass with the world champion of public speaking, Central Division Toastmasters.*

Kasthuri B (8 March 2017) '*Neuroscientist Explains One Concept in 5 Levels of Difficulty*' https://www.youtube.com/watch?v=opqIa5Jiwuw, *WIRED, YouTube*, accessed 5 January 2021.

Kerr F (2013) *Creating and Leading Adaptive Organisations: the nature and practice of emergent logic.* Thesis. http://hdl.handle.net/2440/91144

Kerr F, Maze, L (20) '*The Art and Science of Looking up: Transforming our brains, bodies, relationships and experience of the world by the simple act of looking up*'

Bibliography

Kerr F, Wiechula R, Feo R, Schultz T, Kitson A (2016) *The neurophysiology of human touch and eye gaze and its effects on therapeutic relationships and healing: a scoping review protocol*, JBI Database of Systematic Reviews and Implementation Reports [Internet]. 2016.Available from: http://ovidsp.ovid.com/ovidweb.cgi?T=JS&CSC=Y&NEWS=N&PAGE=fulltext&D=jbi&AN=JBI15238

Kerr F (1 Oct 2015) *'Changing Our Minds: How great leaders rewire brains'* https://www.youtube.com/watch?v=q6GvsIEOofs&t=56s, *Wired for Wonder, YouTube, accessed 23 August 2019.*

Kerr F (20 Jan 2017) *'How Leaders Change Brains and Win Hearts'* https://www.youtube.com/watch?v=HPD_5y_Fxhg, *TEDx Talks, YouTube, accessed 23 July 2019.*

Kerr F (15 Dec 2016) *'Look Into My Eyes'* https://www.youtube.com/watch?v=019Z0dAzNsQ, *TEDx Northern Sydney Institute, YouTube, accessed April 2020.*

Li D (2014) *What's the science behind a smile?* https://www.britishcouncil.org/voices-magazine/famelab-whats-science-behind-smile, *British Council website, accessed on 13 February 2020.*

Molloy C (2019) *Mastering Body Language for Influence & Authority workshop,* Speakers Institute

Montopoli J (2017) *Public Speaking Anxiety and Fear of Brain Freezes* https://nationalsocialanxietycenter.com/2017/02/20/public-speaking-and-fear-of-brain-freezes/, National Social Anxiety Centre website, accessed 23 February 2020.

Moore M (21 December 2017) *'The Power of Three'* https://www.youtube.com/watch?v=o1jm-2WfTvk, *TEDxHardingU, YouTube, accessed 21 May 2020.*

Pienaar K et al. (2016) *A Toastmasters Guide to Speech Evaluation (PDF)* https://www.toastmastersa.org/resources.html, *Toastmasters South Australia website, 20 November 2020*

Sinek, S (2011) *Start With Why: How Great Leaders Inspire Everyone To Take Action*, Penguin

Sinek S (Sep 2009) 'How Great Leaders Inspire Action' https://www.ted.com/talks/simon_sinek_how_great_leaders_inspire_action, *TEDxPuget Sound, TED.com website, accessed 11 July 2019.*

Sinek S (17 May 2018) 'Nervous vs. Excited' https://www.youtube.com/watch?v=0SUTInEaQ3Q, *Simon Sinek, YouTube, accessed December 2020.*

Vaden R (2014) *Voice workshop, Toastmasters District Convention*

Van Edwards V *(28 June 2017)* 'You Are Contagious' *https://www.youtube.com/watch?v=cef35Fk7YD8, TEDxLondon, YouTube, accessed January 2021.*

Waldon B (2019) *Inspirational Leadership Workshop, Contender Charlie.*

www.ingramcontent.com/pod-product-compliance
Lightning Source LLC
LaVergne TN
LVHW051554070426
835507LV00021B/2575